EASY ONGLAZE TECHNIQUES
for
China Painters and Potters

'Red poppy bowl' — 23 cm: brushwork with a stencil

EASY ONGLAZE TECHNIQUES

for
China Painters and Potters

HEATHER TAILOR

Acknowledgments

I am indebted to my talented friend Helen Jones for her generous suggestions and editorial skill.
To my two sons, Andrew and Paul, and my husband Bob, thank you for helping me with the photography.

Photography by Heather Tailor

Cover: *'Pear Bowl' — 30 cm bowl, metallics on black ceramic (Chapter 10)*

Published in Great Britain 1997
A & C Black (Publishers) Limited
35 Bedford Row, London WC1R 4JH
ISBN 0 7136 4726 4

Contents

Introduction

This is a 'quick and easy' era where furniture comes in flat boxes and is assembled in minutes, lawns come in a roll and are laid in hours and every conceivable labour-saving device is available. It is not surprising that art students expect to learn faster and produce results. Time is money and even the TAFE art courses I teach in Western Australia have a time-frame on learning. How can a lecturer teach students to paint on china in fifty-two hours? This book is the result of that experience. Onglaze painting has many facets and there are hundreds of techniques and styles, not to mention the sheer diversity of surfaces and ware. This is part of its magic; experimenting, learning and overcoming new challenges. This book deals only with one small area—the easy techniques—and it has been written with beginners in mind, but I am sure experienced china painters will also enjoy the contents.

Heather Tailor 1992

1 The Origins of Onglaze Painting

Porcelain was discovered by the Chinese during the T'ang period (618-906 AD) but Europe remained ignorant of its existence until the sixteenth century.

Pottery in Europe at that time was quite coarse earthenware used only by peasants. The wealthy ate from silver, gold and pewter dishes. Chinese porcelain was imported into Europe via the Dutch East India trade routes and this fine white translucent ware decorated with colourful designs was so popular that the Europeans strived to produce similar ware. The search took two hundred years. In 1708 Bottger, a German chemist, made the first white porcelain at Meissen in Germany. Within a few years, factories had sprung up all over Europe and the manufacture of porcelain became a new industry. The new ware was called 'china' after its place of origin.

In England Josiah Spode made a different version of porcelain by adding bones to the ingredients. This porcelain became known as bone china.

The eighteenth century was an era of elaborate decoration; the furniture was carved, the walls and ceilings painted with pictures and motifs and gold leaf was used at every opportunity. Opulent decor became a symbol of wealth, only the poor having to put up with plain undecorated surfaces. Obviously the wealthy wanted this new china as highly decorated as their furniture, so the factories had to find experienced painters with the necessary brushwork and design skills. The first china decorators were fan painters until the factories could train their own artists.

Early porcelain was far from perfect and black spots often appeared on the surface after firing. The painters covered these marks with little designs such as insects and sprigs of flowers, creating the style now known as Meissen.

Hand decorating is a slow and expensive process and the factories invented ways of applying designs quickly and cheaply. Ceramic decals (transfers) came into use during the early nineteenth century and although the first decals were quite crude, the factories began mass producing decorated china ware. Hand painting continued to flourish into the middle of the twentieth century. However as the decal process became refined and hand work more expensive, manufacturers gradually phased out the full-time decorators in favour of piece work as a cottage industry.

Many of the European china decorators migrated to America at the turn of the century and some found employment teaching their skills to wealthy ladies as a hobby. Why ladies particularly? This was the Victorian era and ladies did not get their hands and clothes dirty indulging in male-oriented activities. The delicate arts of watercolour, embroidery and china painting were seen as feminine pursuits.

China painting flourished as a hobby world wide. Today the great majority of hand decorating is done by hobby painters and there is a competitive industry supplying them with paints, materials and porcelain.

The name 'china painting' or 'porcelain painting' does not correctly describe the art and the art community still associates china painting with Victorian decoration. Onglaze painting more correctly describes the present day art form, as porcelain is not the only glazed surface that can be painted. There are many types of plain ceramic bodies available, including bone china, stoneware, handmade pottery, tiles and soft glaze ceramic. Painting on glass is another branch of onglaze painting.

2 Surfaces to Use

Almost all glazed ceramic surfaces can be painted with onglaze paint as well as many unglazed surfaces. When a student thrusts a strange looking ceramic piece in front of me and asks 'can I paint this?' the answer is 'if it will survive the kiln at 800°C, it can be painted'. Occasionally pieces crack or shatter in the firing and sometimes low fired glazes erupt into tiny pimples almost as if they had been sprinkled with sugar. However, even these catastrophes can be avoided by selecting the appropriate firing temperatures.

Old pieces from the kitchen cupboard can often develop black spots after firing, caused by soap and detergent seeping into the body.

White commercial porcelain, bathroom tiles, white stoneware, bone china, coloured ceramic, black ceramic and glazed pottery can all be painted with onglaze paints.

Basically the surfaces can be divided into two groups: those with high fired 'hard' glazes (1200-1300°C) and those with low fired 'soft' glazes (1000-1100°C).

White porcelain, tiles, stoneware and bone china for onglaze painting

Most onglaze colours mature and fire onto a glaze at 800°C, but if the glaze was originally low fired, the paint will sink *into* the glaze, losing colour and detail. The effect can be attractive as the image and colours become soft and blurred with a smooth highly glazed finish. To avoid fading colours and blurred images on soft glaze, the piece should be fired at a lower temperature. On a high fired 'hard' glaze, onglaze paints retain their colour and crisp outline.

Porcelain

White commercial porcelain with its highly glazed smooth translucent surface provides an excellent surface for onglaze paints, lustres and gold. The colours fire clean and bright and the hard glaze is ideal for fine detail. However, the paint must be applied in thin layers as any thick build up of paint can peel off after firing leaving chips through to the bisque.

Commercial porcelain will endure many high and quick firing temperatures and it is possible to fire some onglaze colours beyond 850°C.

- *Fire onglaze paint and relief paint onto porcelain at 800-830°C.*
- *Fire iridescent metallic paint onto porcelain at 820-850°C.*
- *Fire lustres, gold and platinum onto porcelain at 720-800°C.*

Bone China

English bone china has a very soft glaze and must be fired low otherwise the surface will erupt into tiny pimples. The creamy glaze provides an excellent surface for onglaze paints and all relief paints such as raised enamel, raised paste and Texture Coat. Paint and relief can be applied quite heavily without fear of chipping.

- *Fire onglaze paint and relief paint onto bone china at 720-750°C.*
- *Fire lustre, gold and platinum onto bone china at 680-700°C.*

Bathroom Tiles

Tiles are available in many colours, shapes and sizes with full gloss and semi-mat glazes, from standard 150 mm square white wall tiles to oblong tiles, ovals, round tiles, large semi-mat floor tiles, mosaics and fancy figured tiles in pastel colours. They all make ideal surfaces for onglaze painting and can be blocked together to make murals, friezes and panels. Tiles can be set into tables, made into casserole stands and trays, or framed singly or in blocks to make pictures.

Bathroom tiles have a soft glaze and can be painted quite heavily with onglaze paint and relief. However, when onglaze paint is applied over a coloured tile, the colour of the tile will show through.

- *Fire onglaze paint and relief onto bathroom tiles at 750-800°C.*
- *Fire iridescent metallics onto bathroom tiles at 830°C.*
- *Fire lustres, gold and platinum onto bathroom tiles at 700-720°C.*

Hand Made Pottery

Any glazed pottery, stoneware or porcelain can be painted. Coloured bodies however, such as grey, cream, brown and terracotta, will show through and alter the colours of the onglaze paint. For instance, if a red paint is applied over a grey surface the red will lose its clarity, because most onglaze paints are transparent to some degree. The lighter the body, the clearer and brighter the colours.

When making glazed ceramic for onglaze painting, choose the whitest body available and use a clear glaze.

When painting over coloured bodies, choose darker harmonious colours or use opaque colours such as metallics, relief paints and lustres. Coloured glaze effects can be enhanced, accented or camouflaged in this way.

- *Fire onglaze paint and relief onto glazed pottery at 800-850°C.*
- *Fire iridescent metallic paint onto glazed pottery at 850°C.*
- *Fire lustres, gold and platinum onto glazed pottery at 720°C.*

Ceramic

There are a lot of plain ceramic pieces available in decor shops. Ceramic has a high fired body with a low fired glaze and usually has a high gloss finish, although it is possible to buy semi-mat pieces.

Ceramic shapes make ideal surfaces for onglaze painting, but some pieces must be fired at a low temperature to avoid surface imperfections developing and colours fading.

Coloured ceramic makes an interesting variation and black ceramic can be quite stunning decorated with metallics, gold, platinum and enamels.

> • *Fire onglaze paint and relief onto ceramic at 750-800°C.*
>
> • *Fire metallics onto ceramic at 780-820°C.*
>
> • *Fire lustres, gold and platinum onto ceramic at 680-720°C.*

Bisque

Onglaze paints, relief paints and metallics can be used on an unglazed surface.

The best unglazed surface is porcelain that has been fired to vitrification and is non-porous. Onglaze paint will glaze on the mat surface giving a pleasing contrast. Coloured raised enamels are particularly attractive; they can be used quite heavily and will not chip off. Relief paints such as white raised paste and Texture Coat can be applied and fired, then given a coat of gold, platinum or lustre.

Avoid applying lustres and gold directly onto the mat surface however, as these products contain no glazing properties of their own and will fire mat, losing their iridescent qualities. Liquid Bright Gold can be applied to highly fired non-porous bisque and it will fire mat gold. Avoid applying gold to a porous surface as the solution soaks in and fires an ugly grey purple.

> • *Fire onglaze paint and relief onto bisque at 800-850°C.*
>
> • *Fire metallics onto bisque at 830-850°C.*
>
> • *Fire lustre, gold and platinum over fired relief at 680-720°C.*

3 Onglaze Paint

Onglaze paint, or china paint as it is commonly called, is in powder form, factory prepared from mineral oxides.

The paint contains a flux which glazes the paint and fixes the colour to the surface. When heated to between 700 and 850°C the paint melts and adheres to the glaze. Very thin layers of paint produce little glaze and will fire dull. Extra layers are needed to build the glaze into a shiny finish.

The paint fires brighter than it appears in the powdered form and colours mature at different temperatures. Cadmium-based bright reds and oranges will mature at 750°C while gold-based colours such as pink, purple, ruby and violet need 800°C to mature to their purest hue. Cobalt blue will change colour depending on the temperature and will fire as high as 900°C.

When several colours are used in a design it is often impractical to fire at different temperatures so an average temperature is used. Most of the mixed onglaze firing goes through the kiln at 800°C, but pieces can be loaded either higher or lower within the kiln space to take advantage of the varying temperatures—hotter at the top and cooler nearer to the bottom. Load pinks and purples at the top and reds at the bottom.

Some of the packaged onglaze paints available list their ideal firing temperatures, but on an average, most china paint will fire to full maturity within the range of 800 to 840°C without suffering loss of colour or gloss if fired a few degrees either way. Paint that fires dull and muddy is usually underfired and paint with a very high gloss and very little colour is overfired. Generally china painters tend to underfire and there are many pieces exhibited that could be improved by a good high firing.

Onglaze paints fired correctly should be resistant to household detergents and food acids but underfired paints will release lead, so it is important to fire them correctly.

Colours and Mixing

Onglaze colours are transparent when applied in thin layers. When the paint is applied more substantially the colour becomes opaque.

Most of the colours can be mixed together and overlapped to create secondary and intermediate hues, tones and chromatic greys and this includes paints of different brand names.

White mixed into a vivid colour will make the paint more opaque and pastel.

Black tends to darken and dull the colour.

Grey can be created by mixing a little black into white, however chromatic greys and neutrals are more harmonious and lively and can be created by mixing together complementary (opposite) colours such as yellow and violet, pink and green, blue and golden brown.

Red colours are the weak link in the colour range of onglaze paints. The compatible iron-based reds tend to be earthy, more like brick reds. The cadmium reds are incompatible with other colours and fire very bright and gaudy. When applied thinly they fire out leaving only traces of colour, so all cadmium-based colours need to be applied substantially to produce a fully saturated hue. The compatible iron-based reds will usually overlap and mix with other colours from the same range and it is possible to mix reds with yellow and reds with ruby purples. However if the red is incompatible, the colour will fire out or turn muddy.

Yellow for mixing is one of the yellows especially made for mixing with red.

Buying a range of onglaze paints can be confusing as there are hundreds of colours on the market. Many of the secondary and intermediate colours are already blended, as well as pastel tints. With a trained eye it is possible to pick out the basic colours and, together with white, mix many of the colours yourself.

Colours can be blended together in powder form by putting quantities together in a paint phial and shaking them, or grinding them together dry with a palette knife on a piece of clean smooth paper. However, dry colours do not give a correct indication of their fired colour. They appear light and dusty in powder form and it is necessary to wet the paint to get an indication of the final fired hue.

Onglaze paints vary in price depending on the mineral content. Gold-based colours such as pink, ruby, violet and purple are more expensive than the other colours. The most expensive colour of all is the ruby red as it has a very high

A tile makes an ideal surface for test firing colours

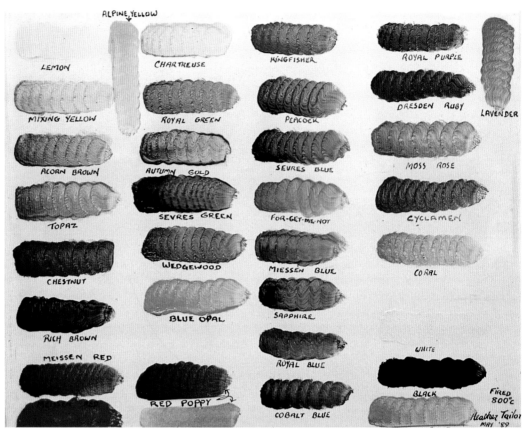

A range of pinks and reds test fired

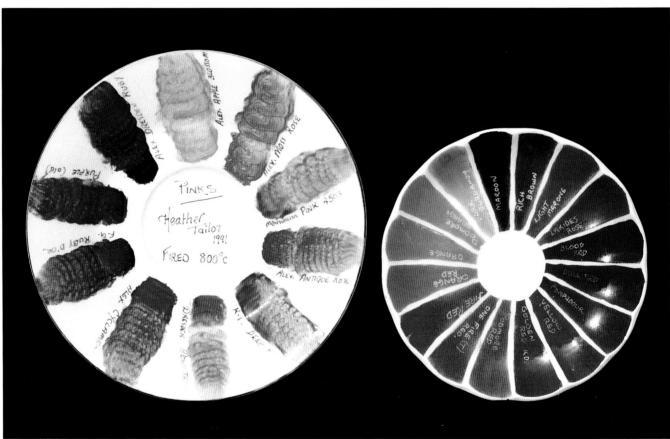

gold content. Add a few grains of ruby to white and create pink. Add a few grains of ruby to a cool blue to make blue-violet and purple. Add a few grains of violet to white to create mauves and lavender shades.

Test Tiles

Always test fire colours before using them in a design. Tiles make an ideal surface for this purpose as they are flat and easy to store or carry in a kit.

Mix a small quantity of each paint and brush onto the tile in bands. Wiggle the brush to deposit as much paint as possible in one stroke, leaving a heavy layer at one end tapering to a thin application at the end of the stroke, so that the colour is represented by a heavy, medium and thin application. Write the name of each colour underneath with penwork, and add the date and firing temperature.

Health Hazards

Onglaze paint contains lead and is dangerous in powder form. Wear a mask when using dry colours. The dry paint can become airborne and be inhaled. Smoking when painting is particularly dangerous. A speck of onglaze paint can be smelted with the heat of a cigarette and inhaled.

Once paint is mixed with a medium into a wet consistency it cannot be inhaled, but can be transferred from hand to mouth on food and ingested. Never lick brushes and always wash your hands before handling food.

After firing, onglaze paint, lustres and gold are permanent, resistant to normal wear and can be washed. It is advisable *not* to use onglaze paint on any surfaces used for food preparation or storage as many have not been resistance tested. Lead can leach out of some fired paints especially if the paint is underfired. The main culprits are acids, such as citric acid and acetic acid (vinegar), alkalis (dishwasher powder) and wine. Onglaze paints that have been resistance tested and can be used on food surfaces are available.

A range of resistance-tested onglaze colours

4 Preparing Onglaze Paint for Application

There are three basic methods of transferring onglaze powder to the glazed surface:

• Mix the paint with a medium and apply with a brush, sponge, pen or palette knife.
• Apply grounding oil to the surface and dust the powder on.
• Apply with an airbrush by mixing the powder with methylated spirit, pouring the mixture through a nylon stocking into the airbrush jar. (The stocking filters out the coarse particles that can block the jet.)

The first technique of mixing the paint with a medium is the most common method of application.

The second technique of dusting the powder onto an oil is called *grounding* and is described fully in the chapter on grounding.

The last technique, airbrushing, is not discussed in this publication. Airborne onglaze paint is a health hazard without protective clothing, face mask, spray booth and extractor fan.

Mediums

Medium is mixed into the dry onglaze paint with a palette knife and ground into a smooth, thick, creamy paste. Add the medium gradually to avoid making the paint too wet and make sure all the dry particles of paint are mixed in properly. Grind the paint well to remove any lumps as badly mixed paint will fire patchy. The paint is then ready for application.

Basically, mediums can be divided into four categories: water-based, oil-based, non-drying and dry mediums.

When onglaze powder is mixed with a non-drying medium the paint remains wet until fired. Non-drying mediums are called 'open' mediums because the design can be reworked at any time. Many teachers prefer students to use open mediums because they can touch up mistakes

before firing. However some non-drying mediums have no grip and slip on the surface, allowing only a thin layer of paint to be applied. Any attempt to build up layers of paint is foiled because the first layer remains wet and lifts off as soon as it is touched. Used to excess, non-drying oils can creep or run on vertical surfaces; the wet paint damages easily when transported to a kiln and gathers dust if left exposed to the air.

Dry mediums eventually dry the paint before firing and generally have more grip on the surface, allowing the artist to build up more colour and work 'wet on wet'. Dry mediums do not run or creep on vertical surfaces and are resistant to dust. The paint work can be dried quickly for transport to a kiln with a hair dryer, in front of a heater or placed in a hot oven for a few minutes.

Types of Medium

Water-based mediums, as their name suggests, use water as a solvent and there are many water-based mediums available from china painting shops. The following two solutions can also be used:

Glycerine A clear, colourless, odourless, syrupy liquid. Glycerine is non-toxic and can be purchased at a supermarket or pharmacy. When used as a medium, glycerine is non-drying.
Propylene glycol A non-toxic, clear, colourless, viscous liquid that can be ordered from a pharmacy. When used as a medium, propylene glycol is non-drying.

Oil-based mediums are made from either mineral oils (petroleum based) or vegetable oils.

Sewing machine oil was very popular at one time as a medium and also liquid paraffin. Both are non-drying mineral-based oils and spirits of turpentine is used as a solvent. Baby oil contains liquid paraffin and is non-toxic.

There are many vegetable oils that are used as onglaze mediums.

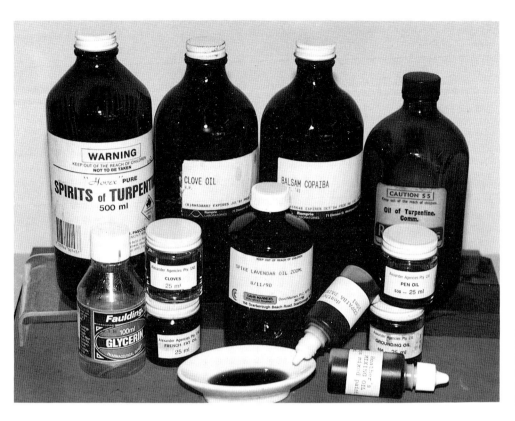

Left to right: *Spirits of turpentine, clove oil, balsam of copaiba, glycerine, clove oil, French fat oil, lavender oil, home made mediums, pen oil and grounding oil*

Balsam of copaiba is a viscous golden brown, oily resin used extensively as a medium base for onglaze painting. Copaiba on its own is a thick fast drying oil, however it is compatible with many other vegetable and mineral oils which can be mixed into it to thin and slow the drying time.

The solvent for copaiba is spirits of turpentine, also called pure turpentine and rectified turpentine.

Fat oil of turpentine is a thick oily resin with a strong odour and was used exclusively as an onglaze painting medium until the middle 1970s when its popularity faded in favour of copaiba. This quick drying oil is made by distilling pure spirits of turpentine. The turpentine is poured into a dish and covered with a cloth so the air can circulate. The dish is placed in a warm dry place and the turpentine allowed to evaporate until it yields a small quantity of honey-coloured fat oil. This oil will continue to thicken with age and can be thinned with vegetable and mineral oils to make it into a smooth painting medium and slow the drying time. Spirits of turpentine is used as a solvent.

Fat oil as a medium is being recognised again, especially for applying strong colour with a brush and for one-fire techniques. French fat oil medium can be purchased from china painting shops.

Warning: Fat oil and spirits of turpentine are toxic if taken internally and susceptible people may develop a skin allergy.

Olive oil is a non-drying vegetable oil that can be used as a medium for onglaze painting or as an additive to copaiba to slow the drying time. Spirits of turpentine is used as a solvent. Olive oil is non-toxic and can be purchased at a pharmacy or the medicinal department of a supermarket. Use the medicinal olive oil rather than the cooking oil, as it is much thicker.

Clove oil, lavender oil and anise oil are thin ethereal (fragrant) oils, distilled from the buds and flowers of plants. They can be mixed into copaiba and fat oil to thin the consistency when making a medium. Clove oil is slow drying and a natural preservative, while lavender oil is a very fine oil which dries in about twelve hours.

Anise oil, commonly called aniseed oil, is another very fine aromatic oil which can be used to thin medium into a more manageable consistency for brushwork and penwork. Aniseed oil can also be used as a solvent to wash out natural hair brushes rather than rinsing them in spirits of turpentine.

All these thin oils can also be used to thin mixed paint down to a consistency that will run down a vertical surface creating an interesting dribbled effect.

Pure lavender oil is very expensive but the cheaper spike oil of lavender is adequate. (Spike oil contains camphor.) All three of these oils are available from pharmacies and health shops.

Which Medium to Use?

Once the onglaze powder is mixed with a medium it can be transferred to the glazed surface in several ways.

- The paint can be picked up on a piece of foam sponge and sponged on. Extra medium is mixed into the paint to facilitate the application depending on whether the spongework is to be thick, thin or graduated.
- The paint can be applied with a brush either as small controlled strokes or broad areas of colour. For brushwork the paint is diluted with extra medium or solvent. Both produce different effects.
- The paint is thinned into an ink-like consistency and applied with a pen.
- A palette knife can be used to apply the paint thickly.
- The paint can be diluted into a very thin consistency and dribbled down the surface.

The medium must suit the method of application and it is often necessary for beginners to experiment with different mediums to find one that suits their style.

For spongework, almost any type of medium can be used, water-based, oil-based, drying or non-drying. Care must be taken however not to use any of the oils to excess otherwise the paint will creep. Spongework can be applied quite heavily with a dry medium and it will not creep.

Brushwork is where mediums play a very important role. Paint mixed with an open medium is easy to brush on and move around. Large areas of colour can be laid on quickly with a flat brush and open mediums are ideal for washes of colour. However, as previously mentioned, a very open non-drying medium can be slippery and lift off when reworked.

Dry mediums provide drag on the brush and require more effort to push the paint around. However, it is possible to apply a lot more colour with a dry medium and work 'wet on wet', applying colour over colour. Wipe-outs are crisper and lines are sharper.

The medium I prefer for mixing and applying paint is a copaiba medium. Although this medium is readily available in china painting shops, I make my own from the following recipe. These oils can be purchased separately.

 3 parts balsam of copaiba
 1 part oil of lavender
 1 part oil of cloves
 1 part vegetable oil (sunflower, safflower or olive oil)
Measure the oils into a jar with a lid and shake together.

The medium can be made thinner by increasing the quantity of lavender, clove or vegetable oil, or made thicker by reducing the additives. The drying time can be slowed by adding additional clove oil.

When paint is mixed with this medium it remains workable for about three hours (depending on the weather) and the paint will be quite firm in twenty-four hours. The paint does not have to be dry to be fired; as soon as the paint work is complete the piece can be put into the kiln, because the oils in this medium will dry out with the application of heat. However, if the paintwork cannot be fired immediately, store the piece away from dust and avoid handling. Pieces can be stored unfired for quite lengthy periods.

Paint mixed with this copaiba medium can be diluted with pen oil or aniseed oil to make an ink for penwork. Spirits of turpentine is used as a solvent and can be mixed into the paint to make a much wetter consistency for calligraphic brushwork, and in combination with clove oil makes the paint run and dribble for interesting textural effects.

Unfortunately any left over paint will dry hard within a few days when mixed with this medium. When mixed paint has to be prepared in advance or stored for any length of time, add an extra drop of olive oil to the paint mix to slow the drying.

A mixing oil can be made from the following recipe and paints mixed with this oil will keep in good condition on a covered palette for six months:

 2 parts copaiba
 2 parts oil of cloves
 2 parts olive oil

Preparing a Palette of Colours

Onglaze paint can be mixed as needed but it is an advantage to have a palette of colours already prepared for immediate use. If the powdered paints are mixed with a slow drying mixing oil the colours will remain fresh in a covered palette box for many months.

Various types of palette boxes are available from china painting shops. They are wide and flat with close fitting lids that allow only 10 or 20 mm of air space inside. The metal boxes have a removable sheet of glass for the mixed paint and the light weight plastic palette boxes contain a sheet of acetate material. Some have a brush rack on the side.

A home-made palette box can be made out of a flat biscuit tin, a plastic food container or even a film reel can, and a piece of glass or acetate can be cut to measure. A large dinner plate makes a temporary palette and the mixed paint can be covered with plastic wrap.

If you live in a hot climate, keep your palette in the refrigerator during the hottest months to stop the paints drying out. Wrap the box in plastic to prevent the odours circulating throughout the fridge!

Colours
Choose at least three hues from each colour group and place the mixed paint in rows with the lightest value on the top down to the darkest value.

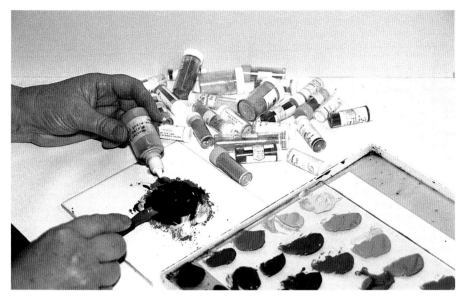

Mixing paint

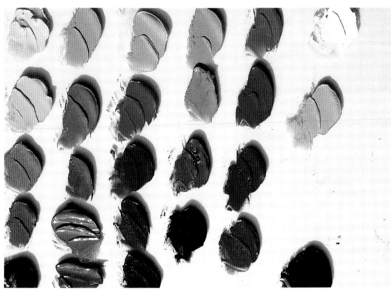

A palette of colours

The rows of colours should be arranged according to the colour wheel: yellow, green, blue, violet, magenta, red and orange.

For instance, for the first row mix a yellow, an ochre and a warm brown, the yellow at the top and the brown at the bottom. If you have a larger selection of this colour group make a row of five, a cool yellow, a warm yellow, an ochre, warm brown and a dark brown. These are general descriptions for the colours rather than the names of specific onglaze colours.

The next row should be made up of greens. A yellow green, a warm green and a cool green, or prepare five greens and include an autumn green and a blue green. Blues should follow, a light blue, sky blue, ultramarine blue, cobalt and a blue violet. A row of magenta shades follows, a light pink, strong pink and a rich ruby colour. The last two rows are reds, orange-reds and black and white.

By arranging the paints in this manner intermixing is easy. Yellows can be blended into the greens, greens into the blues, blues into the magentas etc. *Reds must never be blended.* By keeping the lightest colours at the top of the palette tray and the darkest shades at the bottom, the colour can be intermixed according to value. For instance a deep ruby colour mixed with an ultramarine blue will make a rich blue violet. A light pink mixed with a light blue alongside it at the top will make a light mauve.

A palette of mixed paint eventually becomes dusty and the colours have to be removed to a tile while the palette is cleaned with methylated spirits or spirits of turps. Use your palette as a storage area only and lift out small quantities of paint as you need them onto a tile. Any left over paint is put back in the box and the palette remains reasonably clean.

5 Transferring a Design to the Surface

Designs can be drawn directly onto the glazed surface with a pen or a pencil, however the graphite in drawing pencils can leave marks under paint, gold and lustre after firing. The best pencil to use is non-graphite and made especially for writing on china, glass, plastic and metal, usually called a chinagraph pencil. These pencils are soft, draw easily on the glaze and can be rubbed off with a tissue. Paint can be applied over the pencil and the marks will disappear during firing.

Chinagraph pencils can also be used for tracing. To trace a design onto the surface, use either artist's tracing paper (available in sheets or pads from art shops) or greaseproof kitchen paper. Trace the design from the original using a ball point pen or a fine marker pen. Turn the tracing paper over and scribble all over the back with chinagraph pencil leaving a film. Lay the tracing onto the surface, tape into position and then redraw the design using a ball point pen. Pressure will transfer the pencil onto the glaze.

Graphite transfer paper is also available for tracing. The graphite film on this paper is very fine and does not leave marks like a 'lead' pencil. Each sheet is about 23 × 30 cm and can be used more than once. The graphite paper is taped into place against the surface and the design taped on top. Redraw the design with a ball point pen and pressure will transfer a faint line onto the glaze.

Another very useful drawing instrument for onglaze is a fine marker pen such as an Artline 200. A chinagraph pencil tends to drag on the surface, but a fine marker pen slides easily across the glaze and is excellent for sketching and planning. These felt tipped pens are available in many different colours and in water soluble or waterproof ink. Paint can be applied over pen lines and both will fire away cleanly, leaving no marks. The water soluble version is ideal for sketching onto the glaze because corrections can be made with a damp tissue.

Pen and pencil lines will stay in place while the paint

Materials for transferring a design to the surface: chinagraph pencils, marker pen, graphite paper and tracing paper

is being applied, but the marks will merge with the paint when a lot of pressure is used and come off completely if solvent is used to remove paint. A permanent or waterproof pen can be used to draw the design if necessary. These pen lines will remain intact during the painting process and can only be removed with methylated spirits or during the firing process.

Heavy drawing lines on the surface can be quite distracting with some techniques as they show through the paint, disguising the finished look. Penwork is one technique where marker pen lines can get in the way. When drawing on the surface use a minimal amount of pen or pencil lines as guide lines only.

6 Stencilling Techniques

The term 'stencilling' is freely interpreted to describe any technique which obtains an image by the use of an obstruction of some kind. One can have many kinds of obstructions, both positive and negative. The stencil can be placed around a shape and the colour applied to the middle, producing a positive image, or the stencil may form the actual image and the colour is applied around it to produce a negative image.

Any stencil used for onglaze painting has to be removed before the paint is fired.

Masking Lacquers

The non-porous shiny glaze of ceramic is an ideal surface for 'peel off' masking fluids. These masking fluids can be used for stencilling shapes onto a coloured ground, for creating hard edges around shapes and for borders and bands. The lacquer is applied over any glazed surface and over fired paint, lustre and gold. Applied generously, the mask forms a rubbery skin as it dries that can be peeled off before firing.

Masking lacquer has been used to stencil the design around the rim of this 25 cm plate

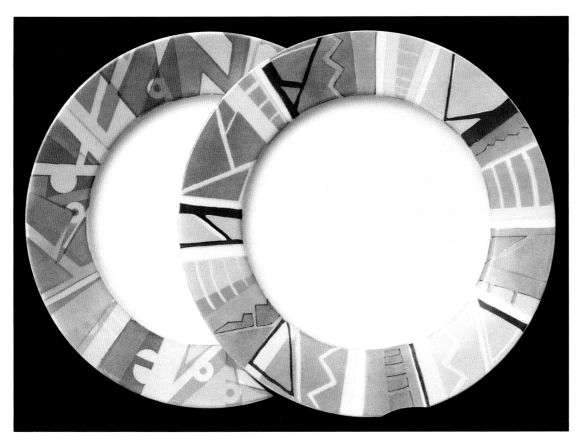

Self adhesive labels were used to create the border designs on these two 25 cm plates

Below left: *Sponging colour over mesh tape and torn masking tape*

Below: *The tape is peeled off when the spongework is complete*

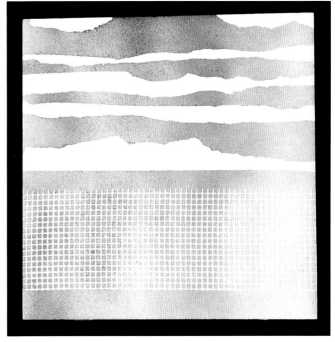

Masking lacquer must not be used over porous, unglazed or excessively rough surfaces as it will not peel off successfully, and although it can be applied over pencil and pen lines, masking lacquer must never be applied over wet paint or lustre.

Once the mask is in place, paint can be applied over it with a brush, sponge or grounding technique. When the paint work is complete the mask is carefully removed by lifting one edge with a needle or pen nib, gripping the rubbery film with tweezers and peeling it off carefully. The skin tends to be fragile especially when applied thinly and can break when pulled too hard. The pieces spring back

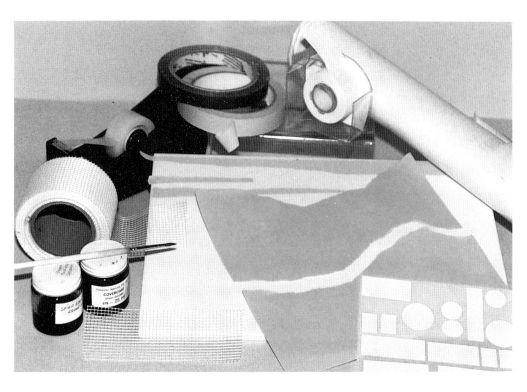

Stencilling materials

onto the wet paint work often spoiling intricate designs. When stencilling in or around a complicated design with masking lacquer, take into consideration how the lacquer is to be removed. If the design has small separate dots and lines, these pieces of masking lacquer could become buried under heavy paint and difficult to locate when the mask is peeled off. Try and join the lacquer film together so the whole piece peels away intact. Any mask left on the surface with paint on top will leave marks after firing.

Masking lacquers are available in water-based and spirit-based formulas.

Water-based Masking Lacquers

Water-based masking lacquer is usually a bright pink colour. Brushes clean in water and if the lacquer becomes thick, it can be thinned with a few drops of boiling water. This lacquer dries at room temperature in approximately 30 minutes but it can be dried quickly with a hairdryer or a fan heater.

Water-based masking lacquer can be used as a stencil for all paints mixed with an oil-based medium, grounding oil, lustres and gold.

Spirit-based Masking Lacquer

This lacquer is green in colour and acetone (or nail polish remover) is used as a solvent and brush cleaner.

Spirit-based masking lacquer can be used as a stencil for any paints mixed with water-based mediums, oil-based mediums, grounding oil, lustres and gold.

All masking lacquers are thick to use and must be applied heavily to the surface. Stencilling fine intricate lines can be

difficult even with a fine pointed brush. The lacquer creates rounded shapes much more easily than straight edges and neat lines.

Tapes

Masking tape, correction tape, plastic tape and any type of self-adhesive strip can be used for stencilling. Masking tape is the most versatile as it can be stretched, scrunched, pleated, torn, cut with scissors or a knife and it will peel off easily without leaving any glue behind.

The tape can be stuck initially onto a clean glazed tile or piece of glass and cut with a utility knife or scalpel into very fine strips and shapes, then taped onto the surface to stencil stripes, borders and bands. By taping around the outside of squares, triangles, oblongs and any faceted shape, geometric designs can be created.

Self-adhesive Film

Commercial artists use a low-tack soft-peel masking film called Frisk Film for airbrush work. This film can be purchased in rolls or sheets of 380 × 254 mm and can be cut into any shape to form a stencil. After the paint has been applied the stencil can be carefully removed and stuck back onto its backing sheet (or any other shiny surface), cleaned and reused. It is ideal for production work.

Self-adhesive plastic film for covering books can be used in a similar manner.

Self-adhesive Labels

Labels are available in many shapes such as dots, squares, oblongs and stars.

Round or square labels can be placed around the rim of a plate to form a scalloped border. Allow the labels to overhang the edge for easy removal. The labels can be overlapped in continuous bands across the surface or incorporated with masking tape to make unusual designs.

Self-adhesive labels are quite sticky and are difficult to peel off individually, especially in the middle of a large area of wet paint. They can be made more 'low tack' by first sticking them to your clothing before application.

Make sure any tape, self-adhesive film or labels used to create a stencil can be easily peeled off the surface before any paint is applied. Onglaze paint remains wet and easily damaged before firing, so it is important that the self-adhesive stencil can be removed without touching the paint area.

Paper Stencils

Newsprint, photocopy paper and butcher's paper can be sponged with water until damp but not dripping wet. The damp paper can be pressed onto the surface and it will hold there for a few minutes while paint is applied.

Landscape contours can be torn out of lengths of paper and colour sponged over the edge to create landforms. Shapes can be cut or torn out of paper, paint sponged over and the shape moved slightly to create multiple images.

Mesh Tape

Self-adhesive patching tape is a mesh tape generally used in plastering walls and can be purchased in a roll from the paint department of a hardware store. The tape will adhere to a glazed surface and paint can be sponged over to produce a pattern of tiny squares. The tape can also be stretched to distort the mesh pattern for interesting variations.

Monoprint Stencilling

Monoprint stencilling is a way of making prints with objects coated with paint. Anything flat and flexible can be coated with paint and pressed onto the surface to make an impression—string, thread, leaves, grasses, ferns and feathers. An example appears on page 95.

The reversal of this technique is to prepare a wet surface of paint first and press various objects into it. Wet sponge work or wet grounding oil (before the powder is applied) can be impressed with plastic wrap or fabric to create an interesting texture.

7 Pen Work

Pen drawing is one of the most versatile techniques of onglaze painting. Images can be drawn or traced onto the surface of a piece with chinagraph pencil or graphite paper, then the lines are penned in with thin onglaze paint and fired on for permanency. After firing the images can be coloured using a variety of methods which are described in detail in this and following chapters.

A pen draws only lines and dots, which sounds very limiting, but with a little imagination it is possible to create not only outlines but many different linear textures. Combinations of tiny repeated lines, cross hatching, squiggles, dots and circles will imitate the texture of fur, feathers, grass, leaves, bark, earth, rock, water, fabric, scales, hide, skin and hair. These pen textures can be used to draw portraits, figures, animals, birds, fish, insects, plant forms, landscapes, seascapes, buildings, ships, cars, planes and many other subjects.

Repeated line work will make patterns for decorative bands and borders such as the designs used on Pueblo pottery and the ancient motifs of the Aztecs, Mayans, Incas, Egyptians, Greeks, Minoans and Aborigines.

Line work is also useful for edging, trimming and tidying other paint work. A black line drawn around a solid area of colour accentuates the hue and defines the shape, and rows of dots or scrolls will camouflage untidy paint work.

Calligraphy is another form of pen work and a pen can be used to sign a piece of work, write the title and details on the base or feature calligraphy as a design.

The pen work does not have to be confined to black and white. Any onglaze colour can be used to make an 'ink', so it is possible to draw on the surface in many different hues as well as liquid bright gold, platinum, bronze, copper and lustre, which are liquid metallic colours.

Onglaze pen work however is impossible without a good pen that works for you and the correct paint consistency.

Pens

There are several types of pens for art work:

Mapping pens or crow quill pens with fine pointed nibs for drawing thin lines.
Drawing pens with thicker bowl-tipped nibs for sketching.
Calligraphy pens with various square-shaped nibs for signwriting and lettering.
Mechanical drawing pens with a reservoir for the fluid, such as Wrico pens or Kemper pens, available from china painting shops.

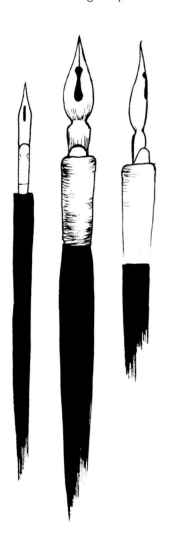

A fine mapping pen and a Hunt bowl nib drawing pen

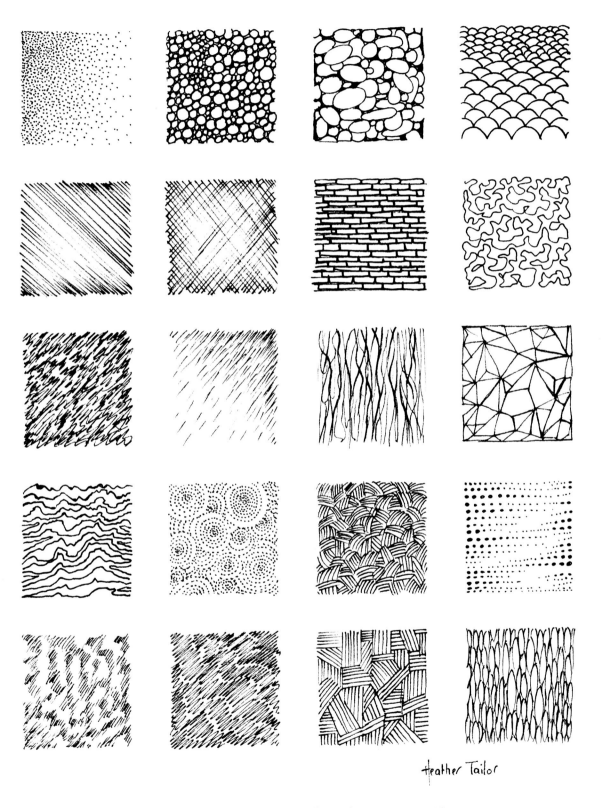

Heather Tailor

With a little imagination it is possible to create many different linear textures with a pen

Pen textures can be used to draw portraits: 16 cm plate—black pen work, two firings

Browse through your local art shop and buy a pen holder with an assortment of nibs to try. Avoid fancy calligraphy pens and aim for a nib similar to the shapes illustrated. I use a crow quill pen for fine lines and an old fashioned drawing nib called a 'bowl point' for quick strong line work. The nib I am currently using is made by Hunt (Hunt Bowl Nibs).

Ink

Mix onglaze paint into a firm consistency with copaiba mixing oil or painting medium. Transfer a small quantity of the mixed paint onto a tile and dilute to a thin consistency with pen oil. Specially prepared pen oil can be purchased from china painting shops or use any essential oil, such as anise oil (aniseed), oil of lavender or oil of cloves. Even a little spirits of turpentine will dilute the paint into an 'ink' consistency.

The correct consistency for pen work is very important and only achieved by trial and error. When the consistency is too thick, the paint will not flow off the pen in a continuous line and the nib clogs. When the consistency is too thin, the line work will spread, creep and run. Experiment with the consistency until the paint flows off the pen easily and the lines are crisp. The paint will eventually dry on the nib so frequent dunkings in the turps jar are necessary.

Application

Turn the pen over onto its back and scoop paint onto the back of it. Turn the pen back to its correct frontal position and try drawing a line sideways (left to right or vice versa). Avoid holding the pen vertically like a ball point pen, try and keep the angle low, nearer to the surface, and draw slowly. Try different pressures on the nib to make the paint flow and once it is flowing smoothly keep the nib on the surface and avoid breaking the line until necessary.

Usually pointed mapping and drawing pens work best when used sideways, so it is necessary to turn the piece rather than trying to turn the pen.

Remember, experiment with the paint consistency and use the pen sideways and slowly.

28

Dot Work

The humble dot made with a pen is actually a tiny shape, but when dots are applied in rows they create a line and when clustered together create a mass. Entire designs can be created from dots, either in one colour or multicolours, and after firing can be tinted with a wash of colour as in the pen and wash technique.

A dotted line has a soft lacy look and masses of dots create a fine grain textural effect like sand. A design completely made up of dots will have a much more delicate feel to it that one composed of linear texture. Dots clustered together and gradually dispersing will give a graduated tonal effect and may be used to create the illusion of a curved surface or shadows in folds and crevices.

To create a dot design, first draw the design onto the surface very lightly with chinagraph pencil. Then dot the design using a pen and onglaze ink and fire. The pencil will disappear in the firing.

Coloured dots can be used for Pointillism and Divisionalism which are styles of art that emerged in the late 19th century and are associated with Impressionism. Divisionalism refers to a divided palette, meaning the colours are not mixed but divided into basic individual hues and applied in dots (Pointillism) or dabs and strokes (Impressionism).

To create a violet, dots of red and blue are applied adjacent to one another. The eye optically mixes the two colours and the combination of dots appears as violet. With this method it is possible to create fields of changing colours that shimmer with energy. Stronger coloured areas are created by crowding the dots close together and shadows by applying complementary colours alongside each other, for instance yellow and violet mix optically to create a grey; black is never used in Divisionalism.

After firing, a thin wash of paint can be applied to parts of the design to accent the shapes.

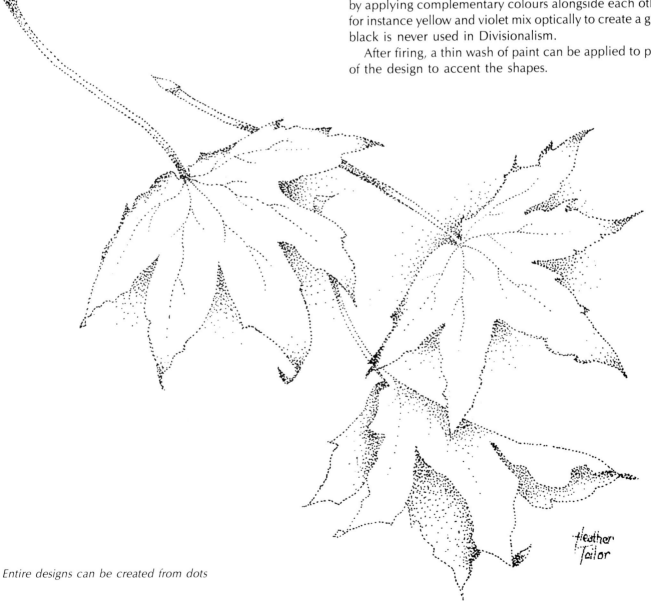

Entire designs can be created from dots

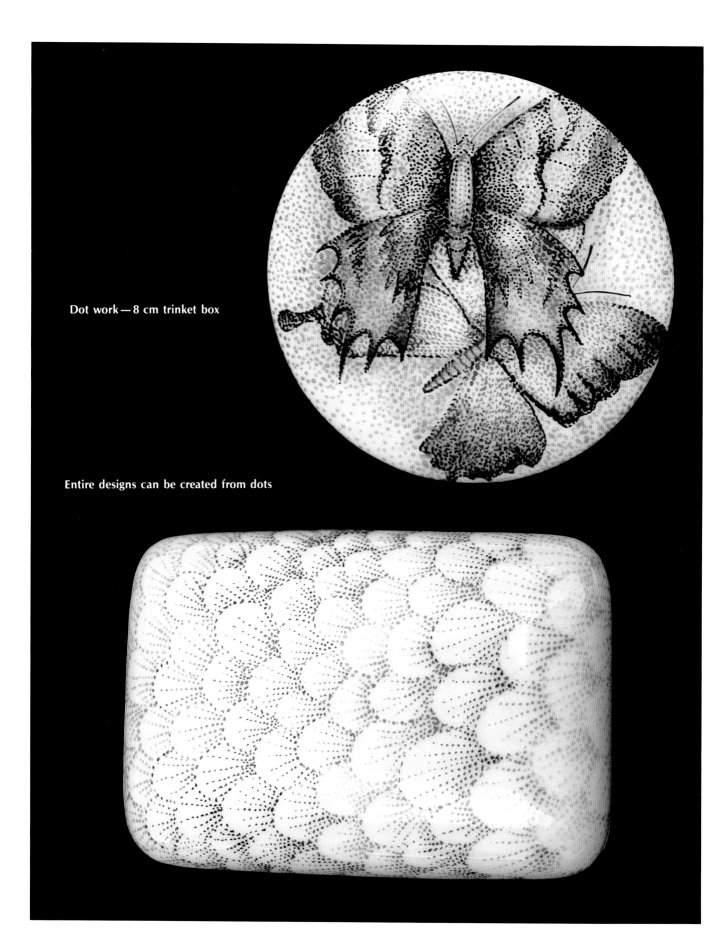

Dot work — 8 cm trinket box

Entire designs can be created from dots

'Strelitzias' — 20 X 10 cm tile. First fire pen work for pen and wash technique

Brush thin layers of paint over the design

Pen and Wash

Draw or trace the outline of a design onto the surface with chinagraph pencil or graphite paper. Complete the design with pen lines, dots and textures using one or multiple onglaze colours. Fire the pen work to 800°C and then brush thin layers of paint over the design to model, shade and tint the subject and background. Fire again to 800°C.

With pen and wash technique the pen work is the principal element and the wash of colour an additional accent to the composition. Brown and sepia pen lines with a wash of harmonious autumn tones will create an old world or rustic feeling. Soft grey pen work with a wash of cool blues, mauves and pinks will create a subtle restful mood.

Nuts, berries, seeds and pods are particularly effective in the pen and wash technique. Use a brown for the initial pen work and washes of warm autumn colours to tint each individual shape with touches of strong colour in the focal area.

When selecting designs for the pen and wash technique look for subjects that have a great deal of linear texture. For instance, a group of trees provides the opportunity to use different textural effects on the bark and foliage as well as thick and thin line work for the branches and twigs. On the other hand a design of large smooth leaves provides no opportunity to explore the subject with textural pen effects.

Wet on Wet

Freshly applied pen lines do not dry immediately and this can be an advantage as the lines can be deliberately blurred in places to create a softer effect.

A design can be created by using brush work and pen work together wet on wet. Obviously if the paint work is thick and very wet any pen line applied on top or alongside will creep into the paint and the thick paint will clog the pen nib. When using the wet on wet method, apply the paint thinly and use less oil.

Wet on wet is ideal for portraiture and any design where sensitive line work is needed.

A water-based ink that will dry when applied to the surface can be made by mixing dry onglaze paint with sugar and water or lemonade. The design is penned on first, allowed to dry, then painted over using an oil-based paint.

Pen and Sponge

This is one of the simplest ways of creating a bold, colourful design. The entire design is outlined first using either black or grey onglaze pen work and fired. After firing, segments of the design are surrounded with masking lacquer, colour is sponged into the shapes and the mask peeled off before firing. Not every segment of the design can be coloured at the same time and it takes several firings to completely colour it in.

Pen and sponge is similar to the black line drawings children love to colour in and the design has to be planned carefully for this technique to work successfully. The design should be made up of large shapes rather than many tiny narrow sections as sponge painting produces solid flat colour or graduated tonings from light to dark.

There are some dangers with the pen and sponge technique, especially on commercial porcelain. Excess paint can chip off porcelain and care must be taken when applying thick layers. Apply the initial pen lines very finely with a thin onglaze ink. When masking around each segment for the sponge work, try and cover most of the pen line with the mask and avoid overlapping paint layers.

Drawing for pen and sponge pelicans

Pen and Sponge Pelican Design

See also pages 34–35.
- Trace the design onto the surface.
- Prepare a black onglaze ink for pen work.
- Carefully pen in the design.
- Fire the piece to 800°C.
- Use a masking lacquer to block out the pelicans leaving the background exposed.
- Choose a colour for the background.
- Mix the colour with medium to a soft consistency for sponge work.
- When the masking lacquer is dry, sponge the colour evenly all over the background. The colour may be applied flat or graduated.
- Carefully remove the masking lacquer.
- Fire the piece to 800°C.
- Mask over the background leaving the pelicans exposed. Mask over the beaks.
- Choose a silver-grey colour to shade the pelicans.
- Sponge the grey onto the back of the pelicans' heads, down one side of their necks and around the wings, using the grey to model the form of the pelicans and create overlap effects.
- Remove the masking lacquer and fire the piece to 800°C.
- Continue colouring in the segments by applying masking lacquer around the top half of the pelicans' beaks and applying a pink colour. Mask around the tail feathers and apply black. Sponge a soft yellow on each pelican's chest and paint the eye patches yellow (use a brush to fill in tiny areas). Lastly, apply orange to the lower half of the pelicans' beaks.

Rainbow Lorikeet Design

See pages 35 and 36.
Using the pen and sponge method as for the Pelican design:

- Trace the design onto the surface; pen the lines in black and fire to 800°C.
- Surround the blue and green areas of the birds with masking lacquer. Apply deep blue and green colours, graduating the paint from light to dark to model the shape of the birds' heads, chests and wings.
- Remove the mask and fire the piece to 800°C.
- Surround the yellow and red areas of the birds with masking lacquer (beaks and upper chest).
- Sponge the yellow on first, then apply the red using a fresh piece of sponge. Blend the red into the yellow at the edges. Sponge red on the beaks, graduating the colour from light on the top of the beak to a deeper red under the beak. Paint red around the eyes.
- After firing the yellow and red segments of the design, mask around the green areas and apply one or two greens.
- Continue colouring in the segments until the birds are complete.
- Cover the birds with masking lacquer and sponge colour over the background, graduating the tone from dark at the bottom to light at the top.

Trace the design onto the surface and pen in the design

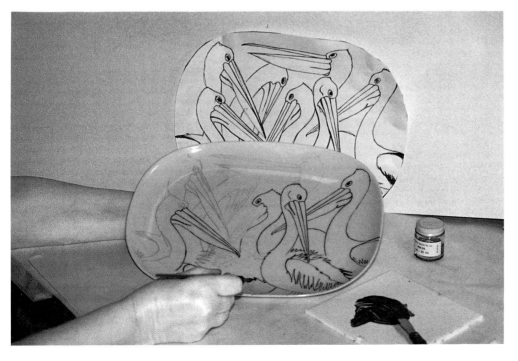

Pen and Sponge Pelicans

After firing the pen work, block out the pelicans with masking lacquer

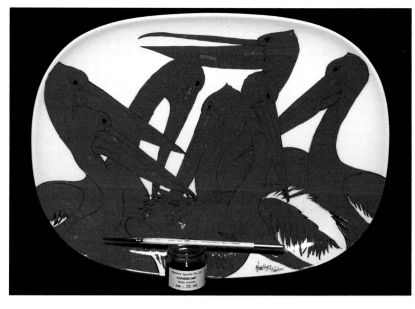

Sponge colour all over the background

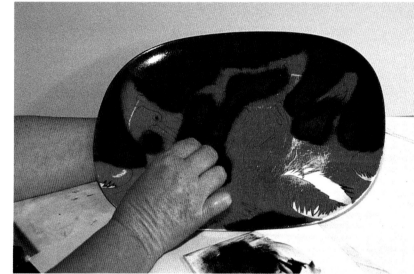

Remove the masking lacquer and fire the piece to 800°C

Continue colouring in the segments until the piece is finished

Rainbow Lorikeets

Below left: *After tracing the design onto the surface, penning the lines in black and firing to 800°C, use masking lacquer to block around parts of the design and sponge colour on*

Below: *'Rainbow lorikeets' — 30 × 15 cm porcelain tile ready to frame*

Rainbow lorikeets drawing for pages 33 and 35

8 Liquid Bright Gold

There is no doubt that gold is the most popular of all the onglaze effects and one of the most misunderstood.

Liquid bright gold is only one of several bright metal finishes available for onglaze painting, others being platinum, palladium, bronze and copper. There are also different types of gold, for example, burnishing gold, roman gold, mat gold and powdered gold.

Liquid bright gold for onglaze painting is the easiest gold to use and the least expensive. This type of gold is priced by the gram, packed in small glass phials and is applied directly from the phial to the surface with either a brush or a pen.

There are various grades of purity in liquid gold. The thinnest gold contains only 8 per cent pure gold and usually requires two fired coats to produce a bright gold finish. A higher quality liquid gold usually contains 11 or 12 per cent pure gold and will produce a quality bright gold finish in one coat if applied correctly. Obviously the higher the gold content the higher the price.

Liquid bright gold is a thick brown fluid in an unfired state. When it is applied to a glazed ceramic surface and fired to maturity, the organic components burn away and a thin film of gold one-100,000th of an inch thick is deposited on the glaze. The gold contains bismuth which 'glues' it to the glaze. This gold film does not wear well and will gradually wear thin with constant handling. Several coats of gold can be applied and fired on top of each other to build up a thicker gold leaf.

Applying Gold

For large solid areas of bright gold use a brush and apply liberally in smooth even brush strokes. The unfired gold should be a deep golden brown colour on application and, because it dries quickly, may appear slightly uneven before firing. However, it will fire a bright gold all over. When gold is applied too thinly it fires a dark unattractive violet colour; so if uneven patches show up in the fired gold film, recoat the surface with another layer of gold and refire. When gold is applied too thickly it will fire black or dull, and it is better to apply two thin coats of gold, firing in between, than trying to achieve a perfect film by over indulgence.

Gold can also be applied with a pen dipped directly into the phial. When liquid bright gold is fresh it is generally fluid enough to apply easily with a pen, however as the gold ages the solution becomes thick and pen application frustrating. Thick gold must be thinned to a suitable consistency for pen work with gold thinner.

Gold can be applied with a sponge but it is quite wasteful as the sponge soaks up too much gold. A sponge will create an uneven stippled effect that can be quite effective around the rims of plates.

Another interesting way of applying gold is to use plastic wrap to imprint textured gold effects onto the surface. The gold has to be painted onto another surface first, then the plastic wrap is pressed on to pick up fragments of wet gold which are transferred to the piece.

To apply a line of gold around the rim of a plate or lip of a vase, use a cotton tip. First strip some of the cotton wool off the tip, then dip it into the gold. Press the tip against the inside edge of the gold phial twirling it around to wind the cotton hairs tightly to the stick and squeeze out excess gold. Then slowly run the gold soaked cotton tip around the rim of the plate.

Surfaces for Gold

Gold can be applied over any fired glazed non-porous surface. Unlike onglaze paint, liquid gold does not contain any glaze and it relies on the glazed surface to fire shiny. If the surface has a glossy glaze, the gold will fire with a bright reflective surface. When the glaze is semi-mat the gold fires an attractive mat gold. Gold applied over unglazed porous surfaces will fire grey.

Gold can also be applied over fired onglaze paint, relief paint and lustre and used as a trim or accent for brushwork, spongework, grounding and penwork. Gold used over metallic paints which are mat and porous will result in unsatisfactory effects.

Applying liquid bright gold. The gold is being applied over fired paint on this plate

Below: *Gold over a soft surface (in this case, fired yellow paint) separates and creates a crazed effect*

Right above: *Different types of gold and platinum*

Right: *Bronze, gold, platinum and copper. The edge of the plate is gold over fired paint*

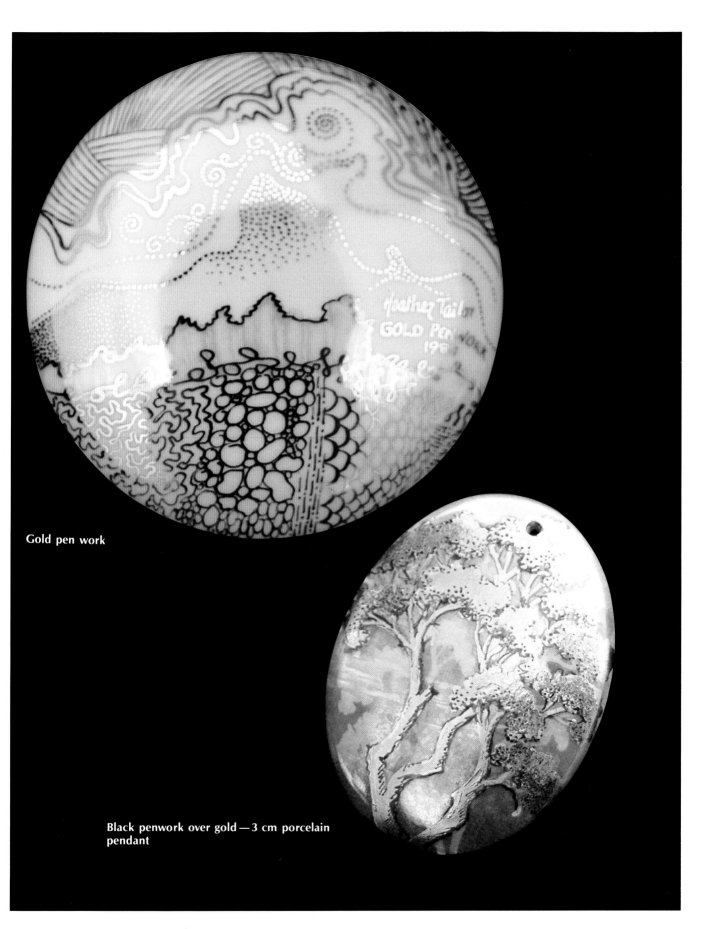

Gold pen work

Black penwork over gold — 3 cm porcelain pendant

Gold fires semi-mat over a painted surface and it is possible to create unusual mat gold effects by deliberately using onglaze paint as an underbase.

Firing Gold

Gold will mature onto a glazed surface from 680 to 800°C depending on how hard the glaze is.

When gold is applied over a hard glaze such as commercial porcelain, it should be fired at between 720 and 750°C.

Over a soft glaze such as bone china, fired paintwork and low fired glazes, the gold should be fired at 680°C. If the gold is overfired on a soft glaze, it will fire into the glaze and spoil. Sometimes the soft surface separates and creates an interesting crazed effect. Gold will tolerate 800°C but only on a hard porcelain surface.

Solvents and Thinners

Methylated spirits should be used to clean the surface before gold application and for removing any mistakes.

When removing mistakes in the gold application with methylated spirits, wipe the surface several times with a clean rag to avoid leaving smears on the surface. Tiny smears of gold are often invisible before firing but will show up as purple smudges after firing. Gold also has a tendency to stain your fingers and it is very easy to leave finger marks on the work that may fire as dark smudges. Always wipe unpainted areas front, back and inside with methylated spirits before firing.

Small amounts of unwanted fired gold can be removed from the surface with a special rubber called a gold eraser. These hard green rubbers are available from china painting shops and are used like a drawing eraser to rub away the fired gold.

Gold can be removed from brushes with methylated spirits or gold thinner and it is advisable to wash the brushes in soap and water afterwards to prevent the chemicals damaging the hairs.

Gold can be thinned with gold thinner which is a special solution for this purpose. Never add any other solution to liquid gold or allow the unfired gold to come into contact with wet paint work. Any foreign material under, over or touching wet gold will spoil the finish.

Platinum, Palladium, Bronze and Copper

These bright metallic paints resemble liquid bright gold in the unfired state and are applied in exactly the same way as gold.

Platinum is sometimes mistakenly called silver, but although platinum fires a dark silver colour it does not contain any actual silver metal as silver tarnishes and is not practical. Liquid bright platinum is more expensive than gold and is not as popular because of its cold chrome finish. However, combinations of gold and platinum in a design can be quite elegant. Gold can also be applied over fired platinum to create a 'white gold' colour.

Platinum must never be overfired; in fact it fires at its best, light and silvery, from 680 to 700°C and up to 720°C. As the temperature climbs the colour darkens and at 800°C platinum will fire a dark silver like black lustre.

Palladium is a cheap version of platinum and fires a darker silver. Fire palladium low (as for platinum) for a silvery finish.

Bronze is a rich bronzy gold colour and quite beautiful as a complement to autumn tonings.

Copper is actually a lustre and fires a rich red bronze colour when applied heavily and a blue violet shade when applied thinly.

Platinum, palladium, bronze and copper should be applied and fired over a clean glazed surface for the best effects. They can be applied onto a semi-mat glaze and over fired paint, but they are not as effective as liquid bright gold in the same situation.

Gold Penwork

Gold penwork is a very useful technique for onglaze work. A design can be created entirely out of gold linear texture or gold lines can be used to outline, trim, accent or work over any fired paint work (except metallic paint).

Gold conveniently comes in liquid form and the pen is dipped straight into the phial and applied to the surface. Sounds easy but unfortunately there are drawbacks.

The consistency of liquid bright gold can vary depending on the actual gold content and age of the solution. The best gold for pen work is 8 per cent because it is a thinner solution. A pen deposits a high fine line of gold onto the surface that rarely needs a second coat even with a thinner gold.

When a thicker gold is used for penwork it often needs thinning slightly although it depends on the size of the nib being used. A large drawing nib will often work with thicker solutions when a fine nib clogs. Gold also dries very quickly especially in a warm room. Not only does the gold dry on the surface, it dries on the nib, clogging the pen, and the exposed gold in the phial gradually thickens.

The trick to successful gold pen work is first of all to find a pen nib that is easy to use with the gold and secondly be prepared to thin the gold with a little gold thinner. Do not add too much thinner, otherwise the gold line will creep. Add the thinner one drop at a time and mix it into the gold with a small clean brush. Keep testing the consistency until the gold flows easily off the nib and holds a crisp line. Keep a small jar of methylated spirits on hand to dunk the nib in when it becomes clogged.

When gold pen work is to be featured as a design, it may be necessary to draw or trace the design onto the surface first with chinagraph pencil or graphite paper. Remember that foreign substances can spoil the finish of gold so it is advisable to use the chinagraph pencil or graphite paper minimally and very lightly.

Gold is often used to trim and accent fired paint work. Gold lines, scrolls and dots will camouflage untidy edges or outline shapes, adding a touch of richness to the paint work. When applying gold lines as a trim, always apply in the last firing and fire low. Gold lines around paintwork can imitate cloisonné and a design can be deliberately planned for this technique.

Gold pen lines are stunning over dark shapes such as black or cobalt blue. However it is difficult to see the actual lines being applied as the unfired gold is dark brown. White chinagraph pencils can be purchased from an art shop and white transfer paper is available from china painting suppliers, so a design can be sketched onto the dark surface. With the aid of a strong reading light, gold can be applied to a dark surface.

A repeated word of warning. Never apply gold next to wet paint work. Always fire paintwork first before applying gold.

Black Penwork Over Gold

Onglaze paint can be painted over fired gold, however the paint dulls and cancels the gold sheen. Black penwork is quite effective over bright gold providing a strong contrast. Panels of gold can be applied to a piece especially to feature an overlay of black penwork.

Bands of colour can be alternated with bands of gold, or platinum, bronze or copper, around a vase. The gold bands can be overlaid with black penwork and the coloured bands overlaid with gold pen work.

- *Fire black pen work over gold at 780°C on a hard porcelain glaze.*
- *Fire lower at 720-750°C on a soft surface.*

---

9 Sponge Painting

Foam sponge is ideal for applying large areas of paint quickly. Colour can be applied in a thick or thin layer, in one flat solid colour or in graduated tonal values of light to dark, or colour can be blended into colour. A design can be formed with stencilling techniques such as masking lacquer, tape or paper and paint is sponged into the shapes.

Off-cuts of foam sponge are available from stores selling casual furniture and from upholstery factories. The grain of the sponge will vary from coarse to a fine grain. Coarse sponge will leave a stippled texture in the paint film whereas fine sponge leaves only a slight texture. Cut the sponge with scissors into small blocks of various sizes and store in a plastic bag to keep out the dust.

Mix the onglaze paint with copaiba medium into a wet consistency. Dip the sponge into the paint and apply to the surface. Try the consistency out on a tile before applying the paint to the design. The paint can always be scraped up and re-used. Avoid using too much oil in the paint as excess medium can creep and separate from the paint, spoiling the finish. Use a different piece of sponge for each colour and discard the pieces after use.

To create graduated tonal values, use pressure to apply the paint heavily then gradually use less pressure so that less paint is deposited and the paint fades away. A clean piece of sponge can be used to lift off excess paint if necessary.

Different colours may be blended into one another very smoothly by applying the first colour in a band, then changing the sponge and applying the next colour alongside and working back and forth along the edge blending the two colours together. Blending very dark colours into pastel shades needs careful attention as the dark colour will quickly spread into the lighter shade. Always work the lighter colour into the darker shade.

A piece of sponge becomes a very useful tool once paint consistency and application are mastered. Sponge can be cut into shapes and used to print onto the surface. Lines can be created by using the edge of the sponge, and it is possible to lay two solid bands of colour next to one another without blending if necessary.

Areas of spongework can be further textured by pressing

'Cat's paws' — 30 cm cylinder vase in sponge painting

42

Sponge and Enamel

Onglaze paint is sponged on in bands and fired to 800°C

Enamels are dotted on over the fired spongework

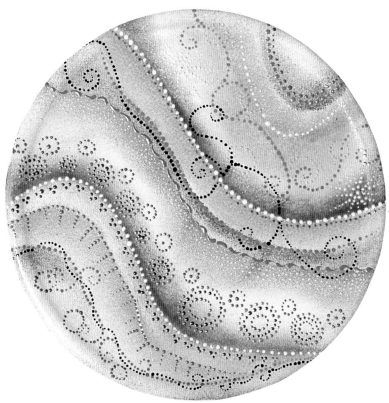

Sponge and enamel design — 15 cm round tile. Two firings

43

Yellow, brown and green enamel was used to accent this sunflower design

Sponge and enamel porcelain bangles

plastic wrap into the surface and peeling off. The used plastic film in turn can be pressed onto a clean surface leaving behind an interesting print.

A layer of colour can be sponged onto a piece and fired. Another colour is sponged over the top, then plastic wrap is pressed onto the wet paint to remove part of the second coat revealing some of the underbase coat.

Sponge is also extremely useful for applying other china painting materials such as grounding oil, lustre and relief paint.

Sponge and Enamel Work

This is a two-fire technique. The onglaze paint is sponged on first and fired to 800°C. After firing, coloured enamels are dotted on over the spongework to make a design. When the enamel work is complete the piece is fired for the last time.

When using this technique on commercial porcelain, fire the enamel once only.

Ready mixed raised enamels are available from china painting shops. Some coloured ready mixed enamels are available, including yellow, pink, aqua, mahogany, mauve, blue, black and white. White raised enamel which can be tinted with onglaze paint to make pastel colours is also available.

To tint white enamel use the strongest hue available so that only a little paint has to be added to change the colour. Use dry colour preferably to mixed colour. Never add too much onglaze paint to enamel otherwise it will alter the enamel's relief properties and may cause it to lift off after firing.

All enamels, whether purchased ready coloured or coloured with onglaze paint, will fire darker than they appear. It is advisable to test fire first.

Applying Enamel

Lift a small quantity of enamel out of the jar onto a clean tile with a palette knife. If there is any fluid covering the enamel in the jar, leave the fluid behind and do not use it to mix the enamel as it prevents the enamel in the jar from drying out. If the enamel does dry out pour a thin layer of spirits of turps over it for storage.

Dilute the enamel on the tile with clean spirits of turpentine to the required consistency. Use a toothpick, skewer, pen, stylus or any fine pointed tool to pick up the enamel and dot on. Experiment with the consistency until the dots appear high and smooth. When the consistency is too wet, the dots sink and spread. As the enamel dries it becomes quite stringy and wisps of enamel lift up on the toothpick, leaving spikes which flop over and give the dot an unwanted tail. The enamel will dry very quickly on the surface and any maverick dots can be easily removed with a palette knife and replaced if necessary.

The toothpick method of applying enamel will also form lines and scrolls. Once the dot has been formed, keep the toothpick down in the enamel and drag it sideways to make a scroll. Lines can be made by dragging the enamel and if necessary the enamel can be thinned into an ink-like consistency and applied with a pen.

Enamel is opaque after firing and makes an excellent trim for covering untidy edges and highlighting areas of design.

There is a powdered enamel that looks like white onglaze paint in the phial which needs to be mixed with a medium to apply. Special enamel mediums can be purchased to mix this dry enamel into a sticky consistency, however for dot work it can be mixed with copaiba painting medium and diluted for application with spirits of turpentine.

Raised enamel adheres well onto a soft glaze and can be fired many times. When it is applied onto a hard glaze such as commercial porcelain it can chip off if it is fired excessively, so apply it on the last firing and fire only once.

45

Sponge and enamel porcelain earrings

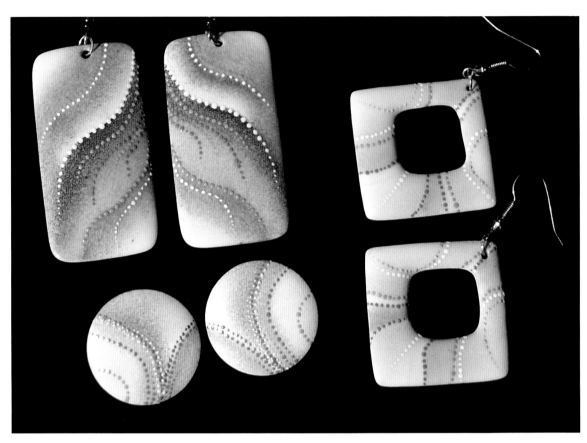

11 cm sponge and enamel box—the design flowed over onto the base and inside the box

Right: *Enamel on a small bisque trinket box*

10 Grounding

Instead of mixing the onglaze powder with a medium for application to the surface, the grounding technique requires the oil to be applied first and the dry onglaze colours are dusted on. This process is sometimes called powder painting and the result is strong solid flat colour which is difficult to produce with either a brush or sponge.

A special oil is used for grounding, aptly called 'grounding oil', which dries very quickly forming a sticky film. Grounding oil is applied with either a brush or a piece of sponge and spread thinly and evenly all over the surface to be coloured; it is allowed to become tacky but not completely dry. A good comparison to the tackiness required would be the sticky side of a self-adhesive label.

Off-cuts of foam sponge make ideal applicators for grounding oil, allowing the oil to be quickly and evenly distributed over a large surface. A clean piece of sponge is used to pad the oil into a thin film until the surface 'pings', indicating the oil is sticky enough to dust with paint. Sponge, however, leaves a slight stippled effect in the oil film which can show up in the finished colour as texture.

To produce a completely flat smooth surface, pad the applied grounding oil with a silk pad until it 'pings'. Use either a piece of fine pure silk or imitation silk; place a piece of foam sponge about 50 × 50 mm inside the silk and wind the silk tightly around it to make a pad.

Once the oil is tacky a large quantity of paint powder is tipped on and gently spread across the surface taking care not to scratch the oil. A plastic tea strainer or small sieve can be used to sprinkle an even layer of paint across the tacky surface, or a whole phial of paint can be tipped into the middle and gently pushed outwards to cover the oil.

To spread the dry paint use a mop brush which is a large soft fluffy brush, usually a squirrel hair watercolour mop or a cosmetic blush brush. The dry paint is pushed across the surface with the soft brush until the entire area is covered, then the paint is gently stirred and stroked into the oil. All excess powder is brushed off the surface and returned to the paint phial and it is a good idea to work over a clean sheet of paper to catch the powder. Any mask or stencil is removed and smears on the unpainted surface are wiped away with methylated spirits.

The piece is fired to at least 800°C and if possible higher to 830°C to thoroughly mature the heavy coat of paint.

To sum up the process, the idea of grounding is to lay down a thin very even layer of tacky grounding oil and rub powder paint into it to create a thick even application of colour that fires solid and very shiny.

Safety Precautions

This technique uses dry paint which becomes airborne when applied and will be inhaled by the person applying the paint and anyone else in the immediate vicinity.

Wear a face mask when using dry paint and keep away from anyone else in the room.

Onglaze paint contains toxic ingredients.

Problems

Many things can go wrong, usually due to the materials or application process.

The grounding oil must be in good condition, thin enough to spread, so if it is thick in the jar, ask the supplier what to thin it with. I use a grounding oil which is thin and easy to apply when fresh. If it becomes thick and unmanageable I turn a quantity out onto a tile and mix in a very small amount of copaiba painting medium with a palette knife. Spirits of turpentine can also be used to thin grounding oil.

The grounding oil must go onto the surface in a thin even layer and dry to a tacky state. If the oil does not dry enough or dries too quickly, problems can arise. Grounding oil must be padded out into a thin even layer before the powder is applied. If the oil dries before this can be done, the layer of oil could be too thick and uneven; the result is patchy paint. Grounding oil that is dusted with paint while it is too wet can also result in an uneven patchy paint finish. The oil will move as the powder is dusted on, creating ripples and thick clogged areas.

Materials for grounding

Magpie Design in Grounding

Magpie drawing

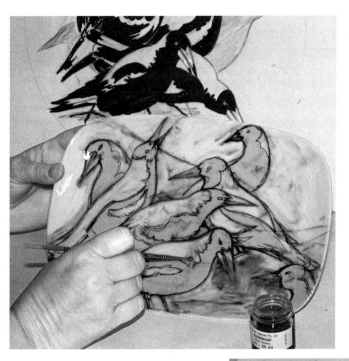

Left: *Draw or trace the design onto the surface and mask over all the white areas*

Below: *Apply grounding oil and pad the oil into a thin film*

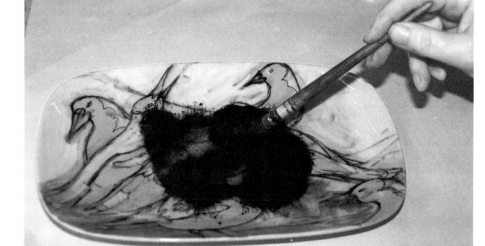

Tip on a large quantity of black paint and gently spread across the surface with a mop brush

When the entire area is well covered gently remove the masking lacquer

Finish the design with black pen work.
'Magpies' — 30 cm platter. Two firings

White poppies stencilled out of a solid black grounded background and finished with pen work. Two firings — 16 cm vase

The mop brush used to dust the powder into the oil must have soft hairs. Stiff hairs will scratch the paint film leaving marks in the colour. Never allow the hairs of the brush to come into contact with the grounding oil. Make sure there is a layer of powdered paint between the brush and the tacky oil. Touching the grounding oil with the mop brush after it has been padded will scratch the surface and also coat the hairs which will stiffen the brush. A dusting brush should rarely need washing; the powdered paint is fluffed out of the hairs and it is ready for next time. However if the brush does get contaminated, wash the paint and oil out with spirits of turpentine, and then wash the brush in soap and water to bring it back to its soft fluffy state.

Lumpy dry paint can also cause problems when applying the powder to the tacky oil. Applying paint through a sieve usually takes care of any lumps, but there is a danger when paint is tipped directly out of the phial onto the surface. Always check the paint for lumps by turning it out onto a piece of clean paper and grinding it smooth with a palette knife if necessary.

Stencilling for Grounding

Masking lacquer is ideal as a stencil for grounding. After the paint has been applied the mask is peeled off. Problems can arise however when grounding with a very dark colour such as black. When the black powder is applied it tends to sit on top of the masking lacquer and the whole surface appears to be completely mat black. The areas of mask that have to be peeled off disappear and small individual pieces can accidentally be left on and fired. Masking lacquer melts in the kiln and burns off, but the paint on top burns in, usually quite untidily. If this problem is likely to occur, keep

'Liquidambar leaves' — 20 × 25 cm tile in confetti grounding. One fire

Part of a three-tile panel of autumn leaves. Confetti grounding has been used on the leaves and background

a drawing of the design handy and check to see if all the mask is off before firing. Making high blobs in the masking lacquer helps as they stick up through the powdered paint film for easy identification. Linking masking lacquer shapes together is another way of making sure the transfer peels off intact.

Masking tape and self-adhesive tape can also be used as a stencil for grounding. Always leave a tail of tape hanging out so it can be easily removed.

Damp paper is another stencil option, but not suitable for intricate patterns as the paper needs to be held down while the oil is applied, otherwise the sticky oil lifts the paper up.

Correcting Mistakes

Unfortunately if a mistake is made in the application prior to firing, it is almost impossible to correct. The best solution is to remove the paint with methylated spirit and start again. Firing a damaged piece is certainly not the solution to correcting a mistake as once a heavy colour is applied it is difficult to cover.

A piece can be grounded twice and two applications are often used to create very deep colours, so if the first fired coat is patchy, try a second coat. Commercial porcelain will only take two *thin* applications of grounding and excessive paint will chip off. Soft glazed pieces can be grounded quite heavily several times without the risk of chipping as the soft glaze absorbs more paint.

Scratch marks and damage to the unfired paint layer can be camouflaged by using sgraffito, which is the technique of scratching an image out of a dry grounded surface. (See the section on sgraffito, page 53.)

Liquid bright gold can be applied over fired paint (see chapter on gold, page 37) and it is possible to pen gold lines and dots over the surface to cover imperfect areas. Gold fires onto the surface in a very thin film so there is no danger of an excessive build up of paint.

Variations in Grounding Techniques

By varying the thickness and texture of the grounding oil and applying dry colours in different ways, grounding can produce many interesting onglaze effects.

Textured and Streaky Effects

Instead of padding the grounding oil smooth and even with a silk pad, press scrunched up plastic wrap into the tacky oil and peel off to create a textured surface, then dust the surface with paint.

Streaks can be made by dragging a comb or stiff brush across the tacky oil before applying the powder.

Confetti Grounding

Apply the grounding oil and pad to a tacky state. Use a sieve or plastic tea strainer to apply the powder and sprinkle on different colours.

Lightly press the powder down into the oil with the mop brush. Tip off all the excess powder and then brush the residue off. By pressing the powder onto the surface the pattern of speckles created by the sieve is imprinted into the oil.

A variation of this effect is to sweep the powder around in a circle rather than pressing it in, or stroke it all in one direction with the mop brush.

Graduated and Variegated Colour

Colours can be applied in patches by either sieving them into place or placing piles of colour onto the tacky oil and dusting them into one another. The result is like a patchwork quilt of colour.

Several colours can be applied in a more controlled manner and it is possible to create graduated tonings of light to dark and colour into colour. Each colour is sieved on separately and slightly overlapped by the next tone. When all the powder is in place, the mop brush is used to carefully dust the powder into the tacky oil and if the paint tones are carefully graded it is possible to create a smooth transition from one colour into the other. Paint can be specially mixed for this purpose. One colour can be blended with different quantities of white for the light to dark effect. Use pieces of smooth paper to mix the dry colours together with a palette knife. The same process can be used to change from one toning into another by blending colours with each other to make the in-between shades.

Blushing

Grounding can be applied over a pre-painted and fired design to create a thin film of colour. For example, a painted landscape that has a thin film of white applied over will appear misty or foggy. The effect can be used to enrich and deepen fired colours on any part of a design, adding a highly glazed glow to the work.

This technique of blushing or dusting dry colour over painted areas was common practice when fat oil of turpentine was used as a painting medium. A brush painted design was allowed to dry and powdered paint rubbed onto the areas that needed treatment before the piece was fired. A very beautiful effect was achieved by painting an entire design in tones of blue-grey using fat oil as a medium. The piece was allowed to dry, then dusted or blushed with a rich ruby colour.

Fat oil of turps, sold as French fat oil, is a sticky medium that dries very quickly, very similar to grounding oil.

Mediums used for modern onglaze painting are mostly non-drying and they never dry enough to allow this type of dusting to be successful, however it is possible to create the effect by applying a very thin layer of grounding oil over fired paint work. Thin the grounding oil first (I thin mine with painting medium; it can also be thinned with spirits of turpentine). Apply the oil to the area to be blushed and pad it well with the silk pad leaving only a very thin film of tacky oil on the surface. If the edges of the paint film are to fade away, pad the edges very hard. The thinner the oil layer the lighter the colour will be.

Another form of blushing is to dust a darker colour over another already grounded unfired colour. For example a pale pink can be dusted with a pale blue to create a mauve blush over an area. The application of this second colour must be handled delicately to avoid damaging the grounding.

Edges and Double Images

When masking lacquer or tape is used as a stencil for grounding, a sharp edge is created around the outer edges of the paint work. Without a stencil the grounding oil can be faded away at the sides by padding the oil to a very thin film along outside edges. This is particularly effective around the rim of a plate.

To create a double image, the masking lacquer or tape is placed around the shape in a narrow band. When the grounding oil is sponged on to the design it is allowed to overlap the edges of the stencil slightly. The powdered paint will catch these edges and when the stencil is peeled off there will be a double image around the shape.

Two Tone Grounding

A design is stencilled onto a piece with masking lacquer and the piece grounded all over with a light colour such as a soft grey. The mask is removed (revealing white shapes underneath) and the piece is fired. Another design is drawn onto the grey and covered with masking lacquer and the original white design is also covered over. The piece is grounded again, this time with a darker colour such as a cobalt blue. The mask is peeled off revealing the original white shapes and new grey shapes. After firing the white shapes can be detailed with paint.

This technique can be used to create shadows for realistic images. For instance, several white flower shapes with grey shadow shapes behind.

The combination of colours that can be used for two tone grounding is endless as long as the first colour is light and the second colour is darker. Variations in grounding effects can be used such as the textured effect created by pressing plastic wrap onto the oil; this could be used on one of the coats of paint or both. Graduated light to dark effects can be used on both coats of paint or confetti grounding could be considered for the second coat of grounding to give a speckled effect.

The poppies on page 54 are worked in this technique.

Special Grounding Colours and Flux

Some onglaze colours are gritty and when mixed into a paint consistency for brushwork, spongework and pen work, are difficult to apply. Metallic paint for instance is so gritty it is almost impossible to apply smoothly with a brush in the conventional manner but can be used for grounding.

Other colours may be too pastel for brushwork or are strange neutral tones that have no place on your palette. When these colours are grounded on they often fire to beautiful unusual colours and it is worth testing them.

Colours always fire darker when they are grounded and sometimes the fired colour can be quite a shock when the piece comes out of the kiln. This is because in a dry state, onglaze paint is quite milky in appearance and only when the paint is wet does it resemble the final fired colour. The safest way to check a colour that is to be used for grounding is to test fire first, but if this is not possible, try wetting a little of the colour with water.

Many colours do not glaze well and it is possible to add flux to the powder to improve the gloss. Flux is a lead glaze and melting agent for onglaze paint in the form of a white powder closely resembling the consistency of white onglaze paint. Add no more than one third of flux to the dry paint and grind it in well with a palette knife.

Flux will add more glaze to the paint, but it will also change the colour slightly during the firing: some colours become brighter, others fade, and flux can add too much glaze and cause the paint to chip. Experiment and test fire first and avoid using flux in any of the red colours as the majority of reds are incompatible with lead flux.

There are many onglaze colours that fire with a superb glaze when grounded on, therefore it is most important to test fire different colours to find the best ones for this technique. Making a test plate of colours is worthwhile.

Cadmium Colours

In the onglaze paint range there are two types of red colours: the earthy compatible iron-based reds which fire dark and rich with a shiny glaze; and the cadmium- and selenium-based reds, oranges and yellows.

These cadmium and selenium colours are ideal for grounding because they need to be applied heavily. They are incompatible with other onglaze colours but are compatible with each other, so it is possible to use the confetti grounding technique to create a dazzling array of bright hues.

These colours are easily recognisable as they look much brighter than the other reds and have names such as Christmas red, Santa red, orange red, Chinese red, cadmium yellow and bright orange, etc. Some of them do not glaze well and fire slightly mat. This seems to be a trade off for the bright colour. Never try and glaze them by adding flux, the colour will burn out completely.

Sgraffito

Sgraffito is an Italian word meaning 'scratched' and potters will be familiar with the term as it is a technique used in pottery to scratch a design through one layer of slip to reveal the darker or lighter clay body underneath.

In onglaze painting a layer of grounding can be applied over the plain glaze or over a prepared colour. The grounding is allowed to dry until it can be finely scratched away revealing the colour underneath. The beauty of this technique is that fine lines and texture can be created and dramatic contrasts of colour obtained.

The underbase colour could be the glaze of a pot, a piece of coloured glazed ceramic, a painted design or a specially prepared layer of colour. Cadmium and selenium reds, oranges and yellows make very strong underbase colours, especially when the top coat of grounding is black. These colours can be used individually, but create a much more interesting effect when several are applied together using the confetti grounding technique.

When the underbase colour is complete (and fired) a coat of grounded colour is applied over the top and allowed to

Poppies stencilled out of two-toned grounding. First layer in soft grey. Second layer in graduated tones of cobalt blue

The poppies have been finished with blue pen work — 21 cm oval plate. Three firings

Sgraffito Technique

Sponge grounding oil onto the surface and pad the oil with clean sponge into a thin tacky film

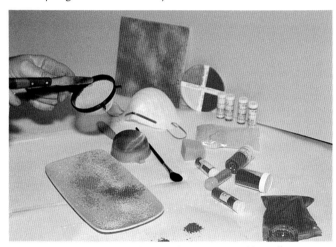

Using the confetti grounding technique, sprinkle yellow, orange and red cadmium colours through a sieve onto the tacky oil, applying the colours in patches until the entire surface is covered with paint

Lightly press the powder down into the oil with a mop brush

Tip off all the excess powder, then brush off any residue and fire the piece to 800°C

A coat of grounded black colour is applied over the top and allowed to dry, then a design is scratched out of the dry grounding with a sharp tool

The finished Nasturtium piece—23 cm

Drawing of nasturtiums for sgraffito design

dry. Then the design is scratched out with a sharp tool such as a stylus, knitting needle, scalpel blade or toothpick.

The thickness of the lines will depend greatly on how dry the paint is and how sharp the scratching tool is. When the paint is carved immediately after the grounding has been completed, the lines tend to be thicker and rougher because the paint is still wet underneath. After 24 hours the grounding will be completely dry and very fine lines can be scratched out. The piece can be deliberately dried quickly with a hair dryer or by placing it in front of a heater. When the grounding is very dry it is possible to draw on the surface lightly using a soft chinagraph pencil.

Not all the dark top coat is scratched away; lots of dark lines are left beind to give the design character reminiscent of intaglio prints, line engravings and etching.

The piece can be worked on for as long as necessary. All the sgraffito must be complete before firing the piece at 800°C.

Before masking lacquers became available for onglaze painting, the edges of a grounded shape had to be formed by scraping away the excess paint. An interesting technique developed from trying to make symmetrical borders around plates: instead of trying to make the edge perfectly straight, flower shapes were scratched into the grounded border and after firing the flowers were painted in as if the spray had overlapped the solid band. This technique will work in reverse. A painted design can be partially covered with grounding, then parts of the design scratched out.

11 Metallics

These beautiful iridescent metallic paints are in powder form and contain mica. They are available in a range of silvery pastel colours, rich golds, bronzes, coppers and gunmetal shades. Metallics look and feel like frosted eyeshadow and are too gritty to mix with conventional onglaze painting mediums for brushwork and other methods of application.

The best method of applying metallics to a glazed surface is to use the grounding technique. They cling extremely well to grounding oil and fire with a mat frosted finish exactly the same colour as the powder appears in the phial.

All the metallic colours are compatible and they can be mixed together to create different shades. Onglaze paint is compatible with metallic paint and they can be mixed together, but the iridescent effect is reduced.

Metallics must be fired high to 830°C otherwise the surface remains porous and loose with some of the paint rubbing off and for this reason it is advisable not to use them on functional ware. Loose metallic powder can be removed by washing the piece after firing.

The pastel-coloured metallics are semi-opaque and when used over a dark surface some of the underbase colour shows through. They need to be applied over a light surface to fire a pretty pastel colour. This frosty transparent effect can be very useful for creating mist, steam, smoke, clouds, fog or veiled effects over a painted design.

The darker metallic colours such as gold and copper are opaque and cover most surfaces. They can be used to cover unwanted paint work, lustre, gold and relief work.

Because metallics are coarse, they can be blushed with other colours immediately after grounding. A pastel metallic can be dusted with a darker metallic or a little onglaze paint for a richer colour.

As metallics fire mat, they are very effective applied next to a glossy area for contrast in a design. They are stunning over, and in contrast with, lustres (for instructions on how to apply lustres refer to my book *Lustre for China Painters and Potters*, Kangaroo Press) and on glossy black ceramic surfaces (see next chapter).

The iridescent effect of metallics is more pronounced on a convex surface, which reflects light to better effect than a concave surface.

Painting Over Metallics

Once metallics have been grounded on and fired, paint can be applied on top if necessary. If the paint is used sparingly, the iridescent effect of the metal finish will show through. Applied heavily, the paint will cancel out the metallic look.

Enamel is very effective on top of metallic colour because the dots and scrolls are a shiny contrast on the frosty metallic surface. (For instructions on applying enamel, see Chapter 9.)

The gold and copper colours can be used as an underbase for landscape painting, giving the finished scene a warm glow. Onglaze paint can also be applied by what I call the 'dribble' method over fired metallics. The paint is diluted with spirits of turpentine and allowed to run over the surface. The unusual coarse surface of fired metallic creates a textured effect in the dribbled paint which is particularly effective for painting trees. (See the next chapter for hints on how to dribble paint.)

Avoid applying gold over metallics, as it will fire black.

Masking lacquer is difficult to use over fired metallics, especially if they have a coarse finish, as the mask clings to the metallic and will not peel off. The surface of fired metallics can, however, be rubbed smooth with extra fine sand paper. (A special fine sanding film can be purchased from china painting shops for onglaze work.) Some of the frosty effect will rub off but the surface will still have a pearly glow. This smoother surface is easier to paint on and will even take a coat of mother of pearl lustre.

Metallics on Black Ceramic

Metallics are stunning on a black surface and black ceramic shapes are available from home decorator shops.

The glazes on these black pieces vary greatly. Some pieces have soft glazes and need a low firing, while others will tolerate a normal 800 to 830°C firing. Unfortunately it is often hard to determine what sort of glaze the piece has and what temperature to fire. If the piece has a soft glaze

Use white graphite pencil to draw leaves on the surface, then mask around the shapes in a wide band of masking lacquer

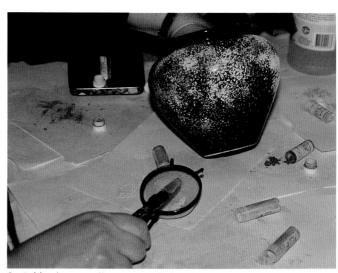

Sprinkle the metallics on until the design is covered

Sponge grounding oil onto the design

Lightly press the metallic powder down into the oil

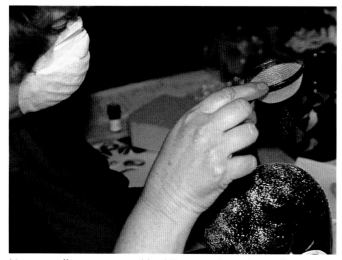

Use a small sieve to sprinkle different coloured metallics onto the tacky oil

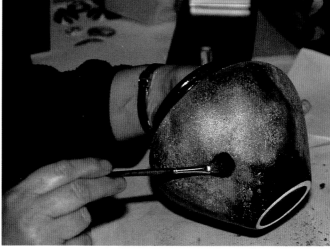

Dust off the excess powder

Peel off the masking lacquer and fire at 800°C to 830°C

Close up of finished piece

Mix a quantity of metallic paint with grounding oil and dilute to a runny consistency with clove oil

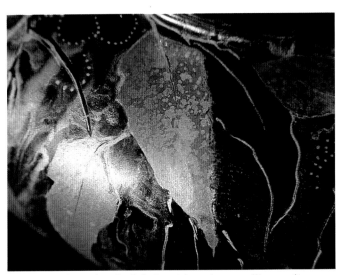

Close up of another leaf design. Note the metallic pen lines and dots

Hold the piece vertical and dribble the metallics down with spirits of turpentine

A tiny 7 cm pottery vase grounded with copper metallic and dribbled. One fire

and it is overfired, the glaze can boil leaving the surface covered with tiny pimples; so always fire lower to start with and increase the temperature in the next firing. Any problems will show up in the first firing.

To draw a design on the black surface use a white chinagraph pencil available from an art shop, or trace the design on with a piece of white graphite paper available from china painting shops and usually used for drawing on glass.

Mask around the shapes in a wide band with masking lacquer. When the mask is dry, sponge grounding oil onto the design and pad with a clean piece of sponge until the oil is even and tacky. Using a sieve or tea strainer, sprinkle different coloured metallics onto the design and press them down into the tacky oil with a mop brush (see Confetti Grounding, page 52, for more details). Dust off any excess powder, carefully peel off the mask and clean the unpainted areas with methylated spirits.

The next step is to dribble the metallics onto the background and this can be done immediately allowing some of the paint to dribble over parts of the design. The grounding can be fired first if rivulets of paint are going to spoil the formality of the design. Once the grounding is fired any paint that runs across it can be wiped off.

Dribbling Metallics

Mix a quantity of metallic paint into a firm consistency with grounding oil, then dilute the paint into a runny consistency with clove oil.

Hold the piece vertical; scoop up a quantity of paint on a brush and deposit it at the top of the piece. With a brush apply spirits of turpentine over the paint to make it run and tilt the piece to control the direction of the paint flow.

The rivulets of metallic paint will dry quickly and hold the textured pattern created by the dribbling because grounding oil and turpentine are both fast drying solutions. The clove oil makes the paint separate and creates the interesting texture in the metallic.

Fire the piece to 800°C, higher to 830°C if possible. A soft glaze piece can be fired lower, at 750 to 780°C, as the metallic will fire into the glaze.

The design may need touching up and trimming. Mix the powdered metallic paint with grounding oil then dilute with clove oil or a pen oil and apply it with a brush or pen. (Fat oil of turpentine or French fat oil can also be used to mix metallics into a workable paint consistency.) Metallic pen work is very effective as a trim for this type of work. The gold-coloured metallics look like mat gold when they are penned on.

Fire the piece for the last time and after firing wash it to remove all loose powder. Very rough metallic paint can be buffed smooth with fine sanding film.

12 Brushwork

Brushes are an artist's most important tool. All artists have their own preferences.

Painting onto the glazed slippery non-porous surface of ceramic is entirely different from painting on paper and canvas. Paper and canvas have either some surface texture or absorbency and draw the paint out of the brush. When painting onto a glazed surface, the paint has to be dragged out of the brush. But there is one distinct advantage in painting on a non-porous glassy surface: the applied paint can be brushed, pushed, swept and feathered into place and if the paint work is not correct, wiped off. Therefore it is possible to paint in thin layers, firing in between to build up the values and colours.

Good brushwork requires a lot of practice and time, something none of us seems to have these days.

Brushes

There are hundreds of brushes available in art shops for all the different branches of art. Choosing a suitable brush in a big art shop can be a nightmare, so you have to know what type of brush you need for the job. Once you know what you require, go to a good china painting shop and buy the best. Cheap brushes are ideal for messy unskilled jobs like applying masking lacquer or grounding oil, but when the brush has to perform exact work, only the best will do.

There are many different types of china painting brushes for every conceivable techique. These 'special' brushes I will ignore and concentrate on the basic types and the jobs they perform. Many of my young art students cannot afford a dozen different brushes and have to make do with two, a pointed brush and a square shader.

Pointed Brushes

These are rounded brushes that taper to a fine point and are made in natural squirrel, camel, hog, sable and synthetic hair.

Pointed squirrel and camel hair watercolour brushes are too soft for onglaze painting and this includes Chinese brushes. Hog haired brushes for oil painting are too stiff. Red sable is the best natural hair for a pointed brush because the hair is firm and springy and retains its shape.

Synthetic hair or imitation sable brushes are a good substitute and of course less expensive. I use a lot of synthetic hair brushes for doing messy jobs such as dipping into chemicals that I know will deteriorate natural sable.

Pointed brushes are made in various sizes and shapes. The size is indicated by a number, a triple zero or 000 being the smallest and finest pointed brush and a number 12 the largest.

The series indicates the type of brush and pointed brushes can vary greatly, especially with regard to hair length, taper and width. Some pointed brushes are long and thin and have no weight at the base. This type of brush is ideal for drawing lines but does not hold very much paint. A thin brush has no bounce and wilts under a load of heavy onglaze paint.

A good pointed brush for onglaze painting should be fat in the belly, tapering to a long point.

Pointed brushes paint three types of brush strokes. Fully loaded the brush will paint what I call a 'daisy petal' stroke. As the brush is loaded with paint the tip is worked into a sharp point. The tip is pressed down first and the brush is pulled towards the body applying a downward pressure to release the paint, then lifted to taper the stroke.

A pointed brush can be fanned out flat when it is loaded with paint and used to paint long wide strokes or short square dabs.

When the brush is used on its tip, a pointer will draw lines.

A pointed sable is generally used for small designs and detail: painting small flowers, stems and buds, blade-shaped leaves such as grass and bamboo; making short sharp strokes for texture such as hair on an animal, scales on a fish and landscape painting with Impressionist dabs.

The brush can also be rinsed clean of paint in spirits of turpentine and used to wipe out shapes in the same way as they are painted in. Painted shapes can be corrected by running the tip of the brush along the wet edge, pushing the paint into shape or making nicks and bumps.

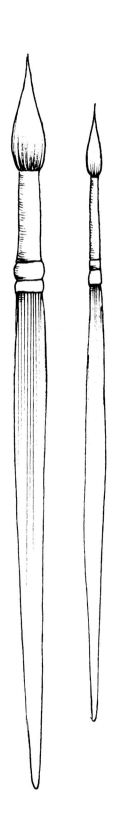

A good pointed brush should be fat in the belly, tapering to a long point

Right: *Brushstrokes made with a pointed brush*

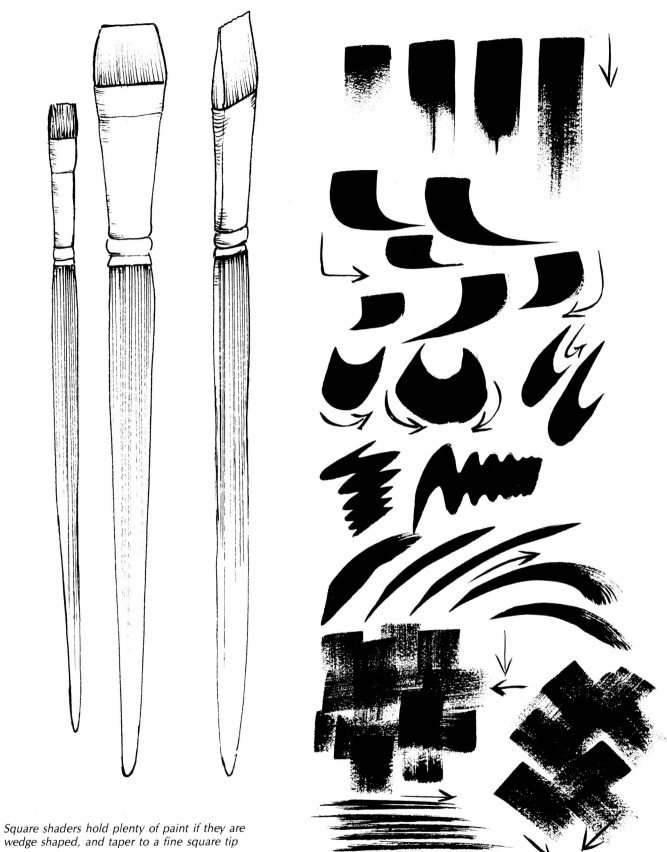

Square shaders hold plenty of paint if they are wedge shaped, and taper to a fine square tip

Right: *Brushstrokes made with a square shader*

Square Brushes

Square brushes are available in natural and synthetic hair. Again it depends on the job the brush has to do as to which hair is the best. For soft technique painting, squirrel hair is the best. For laying on thick paint and grounding oil etc., synthetic hair is suitable. Sable hair in a square brush is very expensive.

The length of the hair in a square brush is an important factor in applying onglaze paint. Long-haired square brushes used by signwriters bend too much. Short stubby brushes are inflexible and only make short stubby strokes.

The ideal square shader should be soft, supple and of medium length; thick in the belly to hold plenty of paint, tapering to a fine square tip and be wedge shaped.

Squares are sold in sizes relating to imperial measurement. A No. 1 equates to approximately a one-eighth inch brush and a No. 22 to a one inch brush etc.

Square shaders are used for blocking in large areas of colour. To apply solid colour, the strokes are laid all in one direction. To create a filtered background the strokes can be cross hatched.

A square brush is also used for painting in large flowers and leaves, the brushstrokes forming the petals, centre and leaf structure.

Loading the Brush

Mix the onglaze paint with mixing oil or painting medium to a firm consistency. Put a small quantity of painting medium in a puddle alongside the paint. Prime the brush with medium each time the brush is loaded with paint. The medium is used in this manner to control the thickness and consistency of the paint. Wiggle the primed brush into the base of the paint pile, working the paint into the hairs of the brush until it is fully loaded and the brush is in shape.

The smoothness of the brushstrokes will depend on how evenly the brush is loaded and how much medium is worked into the paint. A lot of medium may make the paint flow easily but it can also saturate the colour in so much oil that the paint will creep and gather dust. Another problem in using too much medium to apply the paint is that only a thin layer of colour is actually applied, most of the paint is oil.

When insufficient medium is used, the paint comes off the brush in untidy streaks. The trick is to find the perfect balance and this takes experience and practice.

Large square shaders require a lot of painting medium worked into the hairs to pick up the paint. The larger the brush, the larger the paint pile.

I use a range of pointed red sable brushes for many of the designs I paint. In order to apply strong colour I often dip the tip of my brush into spirits of turpentine and actually use a combination of medium and turpentine to load the brush. Turpentine on the brush is also ideal for painting quick brushstrokes and lines as in the Chinese style of brushpainting.

Cleaning Brushes

When painting a multicoloured design it is not necessary to wash the brush every time the colour changes, unless it is obvious that the colour in the brush will seriously contaminate the next colour.

The brush can be dipped into medium and wiped clean on a cloth or tissue, which will remove most of the colour. Try and paint in colour groups moving from light to dark colours, for example, yellow to green to blue-green to blue. By applying the paint in harmonious groups the necessity of cleaning the brush is reduced. When the brush needs to be cleaned, wash it out in clean spirits of turpentine, then prime it again with medium before continuing the paint work.

At the end of the painting session, wash the paint out of the brushes with turpentine and either prime them into shape with olive oil or wash them in soap and water. Do not leave painting medium or turpentine in natural hair brushes. Treat brushes as you would treat your own hair.

Chinese Style Brushwork

Chinese art excels in the area of composition. A Chinese artist would spend days studying a clump of bamboo from every aspect, absorbing its subtle beauty and character and painting it in the mind many times. Then in a few skilful brush strokes the artist would produce a picture. The result was a representation of the subject rather than a copy, with rhythmic flowing lines, intense vitality and interesting areas of negative space—the space left over that is always an integral part of Chinese art.

Painting Bamboo

This project is painted entirely with pointed sable brushes; it takes approximately three firings and is a valuable lesson in composition, brush control and three-dimensional effects.

Choose an oblong or oval shape for bamboo. A tall cylinder shape, an oval or rectangular dish or a large oblong tile or two or three square tiles placed together would be suitable.

Try and obtain some pieces of bamboo to draw, or lay pieces onto a photocopier and make black and white copies in different positions.

Drawing of bamboo

Draw the design onto the piece with thin paint

First stage fired to 800°C

Use a pointed sable brush to paint the bamboo

Paint another layer of bamboo in lighter tones and fire

Finish the design with pale grey or mauve shadows and a glow of chartreuse from the corner—
30 × 20 cm mat tile

Brushes for onglaze painting

Go to the library and borrow books on Chinese painting, especially those featuring paintings of bamboo.

Compose two-dimensional pictures in your sketchbook first. The drawings do not have to be detailed, only thumbnail sketches exploring possible layouts for the stem and leaf formation, where the focal point will be and where the negative space is to be left.

Do not draw or trace the design onto the piece. Mix up a palette of green and gold colours, at least three or four greens, light, warm, cool and dark, and several ochre colours for the cane and stems.

Use a no. 4, 5 or 6 pointed sable brush and spirits of turpentine to apply the mixed paint. Do not use painting medium.

Dip the brush into the spirits of turpentine and work the paint into a wet fluid solution on the brush. Lightly sketch in the main cane, stems, sprigs and leaves with the tip of the brush using very thin paint to produce faint lines. These lines can be quickly removed with a rag or painted over as the design progresses.

When the sketch is complete, start painting the cane stem by loading the brush with a golden brown colour and rubbing the brush into a flat shape. Press the brush down tip to belly at the base of the cane and slide the brush sideways up the length of the cane to the first joint. Stop the brush at the joint but do not lift, move the brush slightly to form the joint then continue to the next joint. A fully loaded brush should paint 15 to 30 cm of cane stem before running out. Paint the little twigs that spring from the joints with the tip of the brush. To form the leaves, load the brush with one or perhaps two shades of green and once again, rub the brush into a flat shape. Press the brush down to form the base of the leaf and pull down or sideways lifting to form the tip. Correct the leaf and stem shapes if necessary by running the tip of the brush along the edge of the paint. When the paint work is completed fire the piece to 800°C.

After the first firing, rework the design by adding more bamboo. Paint this layer of bamboo at least one or two tones lighter than the first application, in either paler greens and golds or perhaps all light golden brown. Paint over the original design and when the new bamboo has been formed, carefully wipe away any paint that overlaps the original paintwork. This second layer will be in the background, behind the first stems of bamboo.

Touch up the first fired design by strengthening the colour on the leaves and shading the cane stem down one side, concentrating particularly on the focal area of the composition.

Fire the piece again to 800°C.

For the third firing, paint in very pale grey or mauve bamboo shadows, as if the bamboo is growing against a wall. Once again, wipe away the grey/mauve where it overlaps any of the other two layers of paint.

Fire again.

Use another firing if necessary to adjust the tonings or introduce a glow of chartreuse from one corner. Sign your name vertically in the Chinese manner.

Brushwork with a Stencil

This project is painted with a square shader brush. A bold design made up of individual two-dimensional shapes is best, such as a pattern or plant forms.

The design is drawn or traced onto the piece then surrounded with a broad band of masking lacquer or self-adhesive tape (for lines, bands, stripes and angular geometric shapes).

Several shades of paint are freshly mixed up and worked into a thick creamy consistency with painting medium and a square shader brush.

The colour is applied in broad strokes across the shape, shading different hues into one another and changing values to create a lively play of colour and light across the surface. Horizontal and diagonal brush strokes can be applied over vertical shapes to create an unconventional grain across the shape. Avoid very heavy applications of paint on commercial porcelain.

Then the paintwork is completed, the stencil is carefully removed and the piece fired to 800°C.

The **leaf box** illustrated was painted in three firings. The leaves were stencilled around with masking lacquer first and painted in harmonious tonings of green, blue-green, blue, violet and pink, using diagonal brush strokes across the leaves. The mask was removed and the box fired to 800°C.

The painted leaves were then blocked out with masking lacquer, and the background was painted in silver-grey with the square shader using short sharp strokes. The mask was peeled off the leaves and the piece fired again to 800°C.

For the last firing, pen work was used to create a lively bubble pattern on the grey.

The **red poppy bowl** was painted in Meissen red, one of the brightest compatible reds available in onglaze. Each poppy and stem was surrounded with masking lacquer and the paint brushed in downward curving strokes to form the petal shapes. The cupped flowers were first brushed downwards top to bottom, then the leading edge of the square brush was used to break in half way to form the front set of petals. The stems were brushed across horizontally and the buds diagonally in light and dark greens. The mask was peeled off and the bowl fired to 800°C.

Then shadow flowers were drawn in and surrounded with masking lacquer. Any parts of the original design showing through were also masked out. A silvery blue-grey colour was brushed onto the shadow shapes, the stencil removed and the piece refired to 800°C.

The poppies and stems were then touched up, the sides of the bowl painted red using vertical brushstrokes and the piece fired for the last time. The bowl was complete in three firings.

The **orchid bowl** is painted in only three colours: a deep red, a green and a touch of yellow.

The orchid spray was drawn around the rim of the bowl and the petals, centre of the orchid, stems and buds surrounded with masking lacquer. Each petal was brushworked in a different direction with the deep red, from dark at the centre of the orchid to light at the tips, and the orchid's stem brushworked in a lively cool green. The stencil was removed and the piece fired to 800°C.

The deep red paint was then mixed with pen oil for pen work and the centres of the orchids were detailed with dots and a few blurred lines for shadow. Yellow was added for the pollen and a few red pen lines drawn along the stems. A cotton tip was used to apply a red rim around the edge of the bowl. Some of the cotton wool was removed from the cotton tip first, then it was dipped into the paint used for the pen work. The bowl was completed in two firings.

Brushwork with a Stencil

Left: *Draw the design and surround with a broad band of masking lacquer*

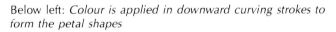

Below left: *Colour is applied in downward curving strokes to form the petal shapes*

Below: *The mask is carefully removed*

The sides of the bowl are painted red using vertical brushstrokes — 'Red poppy bowl', 23 cm

Orchid spray on the rim of a 25 cm shallow bowl

Close up showing horizontal and diagonal brushstrokes

'Leaf box' — 10 cm X 10 cm, brushwork with a stencil

Impressionism

Impressionism is the name used to describe the work of the major French artists Monet, Pissarro, Sisley, Renoir and Dégas. They were intent on reproducing the effect of light on the surfaces of objects, using pure spectrum colours in short roughly applied brush strokes one over the other. This juxtaposed broken colour technique produced the shimmering effect of different types of light.

Impressionism is based on a divided palette technique called divisionalism, meaning the colours are applied as individual hues rather than being mixed. For example, rather than mix yellow and red together to make orange, the colours were applied as dabs of yellow and dabs of red, adjacent and overlapping each other to make the eye optically mix the two hues. To make violets and purples, dabs of different blues would be juxtaposed with dabs of various reds and magentas. The dabs of colour make the subject illusive and out of focus close up, but from a distance the image emerges shimmering with energy and colour.

Shadows are created by using complementary colours rather than black or browns. For instance a subject coloured in warm golden colours would be shaded with blue-violet.

Many of the onglaze colours are not pure hues and pure divisionalism will not work, but a modified version of impressionism can be used and is very effective for landscape painting.

Selecting a suitable subject is quite important. Most landscapes, seascapes, garden and tree subjects work well.

The outline of the design is lightly sketched onto the piece then the paint is applied in short dabs or strokes all in the same direction for uniformity.

The first paint application should be quite light to establish the form of the picture. This is fired on, then a second application of paint is applied, building up the colours and modelling the shapes in light and dark.

In the last firing, depth and shadow are added in thin washes of paint to model some of the shapes. Under no circumstances apply the paint thickly; build the paint up in thin layers.

Small quantities of many different colours are mixed up and here a mixing oil helps to preserve the paint on the palette for another day's work. I encourage my students to mix up three or four shades of each colour group and they often paint with as many as thirty colours.

Painting in the impressionistic manner encourages students to use their imagination with colour. To paint a tree, for instance, dabs of many different greens are applied as well as dabs of yellow, blue-green, blue and red; not forgetting the shadows, so dabs of violet and deep ruby are added in appropriate areas.

Light pastel colours are used for the bright sides of objects and the white of the glaze is left showing for areas of white in the design. Once the paint has been fired on, the colours cannot be lightened by applying white paint over them. Onglaze colours are transparent and white paint just makes the undercolour milky.

The brushwork for impressionism is quite simple as a

Impressionism

First paint application should be light to establish the picture

A second application of paint is applied to build up the colours

In the last firing depth and shadow are added in thin washes of colour

Horizontal strokes are ideal for water, reflections and sky

Slanting strokes create a feeling of movement

small square brush can be used to make square dabs or a pointed sable to make more rounded short strokes.

The strokes or dabs must all be applied in the same direction, as short square horizontal dabs, diagonal strokes or small horizontal lines. The smaller the dabs and strokes, the more in focus the picture will be. Small pieces need to be worked in tiny dabs; only large pieces will carry large broad impressionistic brush strokes.

The small short strokes or dabs resemble Pointillism and produce a shimmering effect. Slanting strokes look like rain and can create a feeling of movement. Horizontal linework is ideal for water, reflections and areas of sky.

The whole exercise sounds like a lot of work and it is time consuming applying all those dabs of colour. However I have found the project invaluable in teaching students to see colour and light and not to be afraid to use colour with more imagination.

13 Firing

Carrying Wet Paintwork to the Kiln

Onglaze paintwork does not have to be dry when it is fired. As soon as it is finished it can be fired. Problems arise, however, when wet pieces have to be transported to a kiln as wet or semi-dry paintwork is easily damaged.

There are many clever ways of protecting wet pieces in transit.

• Plates can be turned upside down and taped down to a board or a piece of cardboard.
• Plastic wrap can be stretched over a plate to protect the wet design.
• Cylindrical shapes can be carried in a similar-shaped box which is larger than the piece. Strips of masking tape are glued inside the rim and stretched to the outside of the box like the spokes of a wheel, bracing the piece to prevent it falling over.
• Bostik Blu-Tack, a re-usable adhesive, is ideal for holding wet pieces in place.
• Some paintwork can be dried off by baking the piece in a hot oven or placing it in front of a heater. The paintwork will turn a brownish colour when dried like this and some artists become alarmed at the brown tint and think they have damaged the paintwork. However, no harm can be done in this way; the brown tinge is the medium burning off (virtually the first stage of firing) and will disappear in the kiln.

Even though a piece may be dry it is still vulnerable and must be transported carefully.

Kilns

Access to a kiln is essential as firing the ware is an important part of the painting process, and every onglaze painter should understand kiln operation. Having your own kiln is not a luxury, rather an investment. Although they are expensive, kilns do not deteriorate like household appliances and will give many years of service with a good resale value. If a new kiln is out of your reach, perhaps you could afford a second hand one. Look in the local newspaper or advertise in the wanted column.

There are many types of kilns both for china painting and pottery. For onglaze painting there is the standard 320 mm (13 inch) front loader. There are larger versions with firing

A large 50 cm (20'') automatic china painting/pottery kiln with a high/low switch and a pyrometer. Maximum temperature 1300°C. The controls and kiln door can be locked

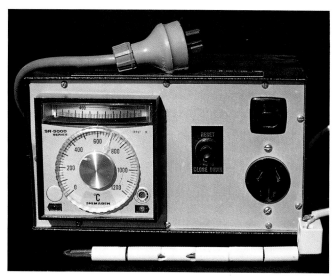

An automatic controller for a manual kiln

Right: A kiln 'sitter' with a cone holding the lever in the 'on' position

chambers of 500 mm (20 inches), smaller kilns with 230 mm (9 inch) chambers and mini kilns that are even smaller. Some kilns are down loaders with a lid that lifts up at the top. Pottery kilns are generally larger than china painters' but can be used for firing onglaze. The size of the kiln will determine the size of the pieces that you can paint. A tiny kiln is useless for larger pieces and a very large kiln is a waste of power resources if used to fire small items often. Kilns have different rates of temperature climb and a variety of controls.

Automatic kilns have a dial which is set to the temperature required. The work to be fired is loaded in, the button is pressed and the kiln switches on. At the given temperature the kiln automatically cuts off, and when it has cooled down the work can be removed. This is a very convenient arrangement. Some automatics have pyrometers which indicate temperature so the rate of climb can be monitored and some have controls to regulate the power.

Manual kilns have to be switched off manually and have a pyrometer, plus a switch to regulate the power—high, medium or low. Other manual kilns have no pyrometers and rely on cones, which are purchased from ceramic shops for whatever cut-off temperature is required. The cones are placed in a rack in front of the peephole and will bend at their programmed temperature. Kilns with 'sitters' have a switch device inside the chamber activated by a cone. Three prongs stick out from the inside wall of the kiln; the centre prong or lever lifts up and down. When the lever is up the kiln will switch on and when the lever is down the kiln switches off. A cone is placed across the two prongs with

the lever resting on its top, so that when the cone bends the lever will drop, turning the power off.

Manual kilns can be converted to automatic by purchasing a separate automatic controller. This device has a temperature dial to select the required temperature and may also have a pyrometric indicator. The auto controller is plugged into the powerpoint and the kiln's power cord is plugged into the auto controller. The controller's pyrometer probe is inserted into the kiln and both the kiln and controller switched on. This system should then operate like an automatic kiln.

Rates of Climb

Onglaze painting does not require a regulated rate of climb in a kiln. The kiln can be fired fast or slow depending on the type of control available.

An auto kiln fires itself and the rate of climb is governed by the size and quantity of elements in the kiln walls. Most auto kilns have been designed to climb to 800°C in 2½ to 3 hours; some may be faster and others slower.

Small and medium pieces of porcelain are very durable and can be heated quickly, so a kiln load of porcelain can be fired on full power up to 800°C in one hour if necessary. A 230 mm (9 inch) kiln can be fired up to 800°C in 40 minutes. However, most larger kilns do not have the capacity to heat that quickly and usually take from 2 to 4 hours.

Breakage in firing is generally caused by thermal shock, stress and weight distribution.

Thermal Shock

Porcelain and all ceramic expands and contracts during the firing process. Larger pieces of porcelain and ceramic such as tall vases over 300 mm (12 inches) and plates over 350 mm (14 inches) can heat unevenly if placed in a cold kiln and subjected to full power. Uneven heating and cooling causes thermal shock. The piece expands or contracts unevenly causing stress which results in hairline cracks or breakage.

Heat large pieces slowly until they are warm all over and then switch to full power. When cooling, make sure large pieces cool evenly and do not force the cooling process by opening the door early or taking large pieces out of the kiln hot. Small pieces are less susceptible to thermal shock. Bathroom tiles are also sensitive, especially the larger tiles 200 mm and over. Tiles are not porcelain and are not manufactured with the intention of being refired, so they can break in the kiln if subjected to thermal shock.

Never lean tiles against the wall of the kiln in front of the elements, as they heat unevenly and can break. Large tiles are best fired flat on a shelf in the centre of a kiln so they heat evenly. Tile racks are excellent as they allow hot air to circulate.

Stress in Firing

When onglaze paint or relief is applied to the surface and fired, the medium burns out, the paint melts into a vitreous mass and the flux adheres the paint to the surface. On soft low-fired glazes, the paint fires into the glaze, but when the surface is a high-fired hard glaze such as porcelain, the paint or relief sits on top of the surface.

When the article is refired the paint melts and stretches once again. Softer glazes move with the paint, but problems arise when a heavy application of paint or relief is refired on a hard glaze such as porcelain. Onglaze paint and relief expand and contract at a different rate to the glaze and stress occurs in large thick areas where the paint cannot move. The sheet of paint breaks or lifts on cooling and small pieces flake off, chipping the glaze down to the bisque.

This chipping generally happens on commercial porcelain when excess paint or relief is applied and refired.

Large areas of gold can also create this type of stress. A piece of porcelain can actually break due to a large sheet of gold, but this is a rare occurrence. Dinnerware manufacturers found that when the handles of cups were completely covered in gold, but not the body of the cup, a percentage of the handles broke off during firing. The

An assortment of kiln furniture and an automatic cut off device on top of the kiln

answer to the problem was to paint only a band of gold down the handle.

Loading the Kiln

Packing a large quantity of china into a kiln can be a tricky business. Pieces must not touch each other and must not come into contact with the elements.

Porcelain is the easiest ceramic to fire as the surface is so hard, stilts can be used to separate pieces. The stilts will not stick to the porcelain but they will stick to heavy paint and care must be taken when positioning a stilt on the piece.

Several porcelain plates can be stacked in the upright position in the kiln, the first plate leaning against the kiln wall. Another plate is leaned against this plate and held apart with a stilt hooked over the top. Racks that hold tiles and plates in an upright position can be purchased and plate racks to hold plates in a horizontal position are also available. These units lock together one on top of the other, with the plates sitting in a well in between.

Stilts can be used to stack porcelain plates one on top of the other, however this is where uneven weight distribution can cause breakage. Always place the larger, heavier plates at the bottom and stack smaller and lighter plates on top. If the weight on the bottom plate or even the middle plate is too great, breakage will occur in the firing. Porcelain is very strong and breakage is rare; however, here are some guidelines.

• Never stack more than five 250 mm (10 inch) plates on top of one another; use shelves to separate the piles.
• Porcelain vases, boxes, cylinders, mugs, cups and jugs can also be stacked on top of each other with stilts in between. Large stilts can be used to straddle the mouth of one piece and another piece placed on top.
• Long thin pieces of stilt called saddles can be purchased and these are ideal for bridging the wide mouth of a trinket box and placing the lid on top.
• Kiln shelves with props to separate pieces are very useful. The props can be purchased as solid cylinders of various lengths or castellated props that interlock can be used. There are many items of kiln furniture available in ceramic shops to make stacking easier.
• Soft-glaze pieces must not be stilted as the stilts will stick to the glaze and mark it. Plate racks are ideal for firing quantities of soft-glaze plates; shelves help to separate the pieces in layers and plates can be leaned against the side of the kiln. Each piece must be loaded into the kiln without touching.
• Bathroom tiles have a soft glaze and must not be stilted or leaned against the side of the kiln. Tile racks can be purchased which take 10 or 12 tiles of the same size and plate racks that hold plates upright can also be used. Tiles can be laid flat on shelves and it is possible to fire four

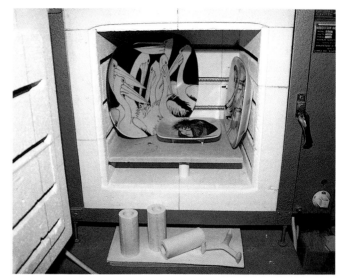

Porcelain plates that are too large to be laid flat on a kiln shelf can be stood upright across the kiln chamber. Note a shelf has been put into the kiln to lift the pieces off the floor

150 mm (6 X 6 inch) tiles on a 300 mm (12 inch) shelf with a stilt placed in the middle of the shelf to support another tile or a plate above the tiles.

Thimbles are small conical pieces of kiln furniture that fit inside one another. Each thimble has a small arm which forms a ledge. Thimbles can be placed around a tile to support it, then another set of thimbles slotted on top of the first set and another tile placed on the ledges and so on, building up a rack of tiles.
• Some very soft glaze pieces can stick to the shelves especially if the glaze reaches to the foot and over the bottom of the ware. Most ceramic pieces have an unglazed rim around the base, but if the glaze is not broken by this rim, use a stilt to lift the piece off the kiln shelf or floor.

Maturing the Paint

The firing chamber of a hobby kiln will heat unevenly, especially a large kiln and front loaders with only three walls of elements. The pyrometer probe measures the air temperature in its immediate vicinity; air temperature will be slightly hotter above the probe and slightly cooler below. The coldest part of the kiln is near the door on the floor below the elements. The hottest part of the kiln is at the very top.

Ceramic in the process of being fired will have a slightly lower temperature than air temperature, especially in a fast-firing situation. So if the kiln is registering 800°C the china next to the probe will be at about 790°C, the china above at about 800°C and the china below anything from 780°C to 750°C on the floor. These estimations are only guesswork

Saddles and large stilts can be used to stack cylindrical pieces one on top of the other

Two types of tile rack for 150 mm square tiles

Shelves can be used to separate piles of work to be fired. This kiln is a standard 32 cm (13") automatic with a maximum firing temperature of 1000°C

and obviously kilns will differ greatly. Down-loading kilns heat more evenly because they have elements on all sides, but the base of the kiln will be cooler than the top. Shelves also block heat, especially at the bottom.

When loading a kiln take the levels into consideration and place items that need a cooler fire at the bottom and items that require a hotter fire at the top.

Firing time can effect the maturity of the paint. If the kiln is fired rapidly to 800°C in one hour and allowed to cool immediately the china inside never reaches that temperature and the paint does not mature. Immature paint is dull and muddy. With fast-firing kilns, compensate by firing 10 or 20°C higher.

A slow kiln will mature the paint but it can also overfire. It usually heats up to about 600°C fairly quickly then slows down as it struggles to maintain the rate of climb, especially if the bungs are left open, allowing the heat to escape. The last part of the firing takes longer and the china has more time to 'soak' and mature the paint.

- When firing slow, fire low.
- When firing fast, fire high.

Learning to use your own kiln is part of the onglaze process, as every kiln fires differently and pyrometers and auto controllers are not always accurate. Pryometers may read 800°C, but the temperature inside the kiln may be above or below. Students often bring me underfired work and claim they have fired at 800°C. Usually the pyrometer is faulty and needs adjusting or with an auto controller a further 20°C has to be added on.

My advice is to *experiment* with your kiln and if the paint is not glazing properly fire 10 to 20°C higher; if the paint is fading fire 10 to 20°C lower.

14 Design for Onglaze

To succeed in any art form a student must be able to draw adequately and have a good knowledge of art and design. In the course of learning, a beginner will pick up basic composition knowledge unique to onglaze painting as well as technique, brush skills and a certain amount of colour harmony, but without drawing and design skills, a student will not be able to develop individual designs successfully. Design is time consuming and requires discipline and patience to develop original concepts, one of the main reasons few painters bother to create their own designs. It is so much easier to find a picture to copy.

Realism and Abstraction

In the deep recesses of our brain we have a visual recall mechanism. So incredible is our visual recall that we can remember places and incidents that may have happened years ago. We remember designs and styles and can recall the images of thousands of objects, plants and animals. During our lifetime we form likes and dislikes associated with particular places, incidents and objects. This is called 'conditioning' and it affects the way we perceive art.

When we look at a picture we have never seen before, the images we see are instantly compared to our visual recall to ascertain if they compare favourably with our perception of that subject. Most people feel comfortable with realism, but photo-realism can become boring because we are faced with real images every day of our lives and there is nothing different about them.

Pictures that are out of proportion, not in perspective, tonally incorrect and discordant are generally disliked because we know from visual recall that the images are wrong and inconsistent. Stylised realism is the most popular type of contemporary art because the images still resemble real objects but are different in an interesting way.

When the images in a picture no longer represent anything real and there are no visual recollections to make a comparison with, our eyes explore the new images taking in line, shape, texture, tone and colour. Often we try and slot the abstract into visual recall by thinking it reminds us of something we have seen, but usually a pure abstract picture is commended or disliked for its design elements and originality.

Abstraction

Abstraction is the simplification of forms. There are many degrees of abstraction, beginning with the slight modification of natural realistic subjects and running to pure abstraction when the forms become unrecognisable.

The process of abstraction starts with drawing and because it is impossible to draw everything exactly, an artist unconsciously abstracts. The process is probably easier to understand if you think of abstraction as 'adding and subtracting' from realism. Subconsciously we only draw what we want to see, eliminating the bits we dislike or cannot draw and adding our own version of the subject.

When an artist deliberately sets out to abstract it becomes a more calculated process and there are a number of ways to abstract a realistic subject. The form can be simplified, distorted, elongated, extended, turned, twisted, inverted. Features can be exaggerated, invented or borrowed; the lines and angles made more cubic or curvilinear. The aim of abstraction is decided upon by the artist; perhaps it is to make the shape more dramatic, the space more dynamic or give the lines more energy. Each artist abstracts in his own style, and so this type of abstraction is called *stylising*.

The abstracting can continue until all recognisable features are removed and the design becomes *non-figurative* or *non-objective*, the terms for unrecognisable forms.

How to Stylise

Using outline, draw the subject in pencil, selecting only the most important parts and simplifying unnecessary detail. Then rework the drawing by going over the original design again. If the approach is to be cubic, straighten the lines and sharpen the angles. Angles are more dynamic and energetic. If the approach is to be curvilinear, exaggerate the curves and make the lines rhythmic and flowing. Emphasise interesting features and if necessary add extra shapes and lines to the design.

Stylised images can convey a variety of feelings: grace, energy, torment, movement, stillness, sadness and humour. As an artist's skill develops this occurs subconsciously, becoming an expression of individuality.

These poppies have been stylised. The angles are more dynamic and the curves are exaggerated

Symmetrical balance

Asymmetrical balance

Composition

The visual area of a piece to be decorated will be either a flat two-dimensional field such as a plate, tile, plaque or panel, or a curved surface such as a cylinder, box or bowl.

Flat two-dimensional areas are much easier to design for than cylindrical surfaces because the whole design is visible at all times and often there is only one viewing angle, as in the case of a framed tile or a plate propped up on a stand. However when a plate is to be displayed flat and viewed from above at any angle, the design has to compensate.

Three-dimensional pieces such as cylinder vases may well be viewed from all sides, with only part of the design visible each time owing to the curvature of the piece. To

Closed form

Open form

compensate, the design has to appear balanced from any angle.

Once the area to be painted is identified on a piece, the subject will occupy what is called positive space and the blank area remaining is referred to as negative space. Both are very important in a composition. Symmetrical balance involves an even distribution of negative space to both sides, with the image placed in the middle; this can create a very monotonous effect. Asymmetrical balance is obtained by placing an image to one side and closer to the top or bottom, an arrangement which tends to produce much more interesting areas of negative space.

When a subject is completely enclosed within the viewing area and surrounded by negative space, the design is referred to as 'closed form'. To make the composition more dramatic and interesting, parts of the subject can disappear at the edges, top or bottom. This type of composition is called 'open form' because there is a suggestion of continuity to the design.

Space

The blank area to be decorated is called 'space' and the design 'occupies space'. A design that occupies most of the space can create a crowded squashed feeling and a small design in the middle of a large space can look lost and insignificant.

Position within the space is important. Objects placed low on the picture plane will appear to be closer to the viewer while objects placed higher up will appear to be further away.

The painting area or space on a piece of ceramic is two-dimensional; an artist can work in only two directions, up and down or side to side. Three-dimensional illusion, giving the subject perspective, is created by overlap, diminishing size, position and tone.

• Overlap creates the illusion of shallow space, meaning that the objects appear close together one behind the other.
• Deep space is created by diminishing size, fading colour values, indistinct forms and the objects being higher on the picture plane. In landscape painting this is called atmospheric perspective.

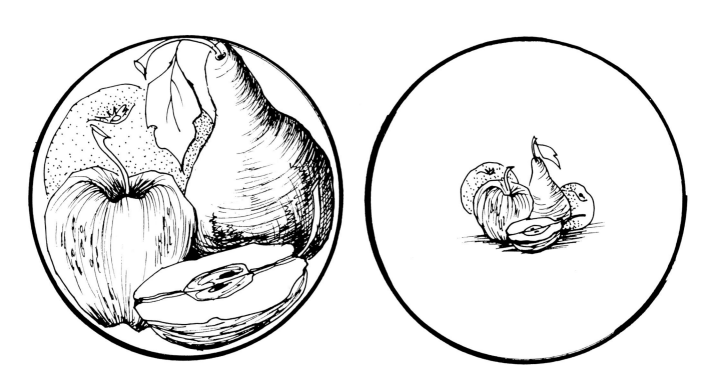

A design that occupies most of the space can create a squashed feeling, and a small design in the middle of a large space can look lost and insignificant

Atmospheric perspective

When planning a design, be aware of the space and what space will do to your image. Do not be afraid to leave spaces undecorated. When I plan a design, I try and leave three areas of space in the composition, a large area, a medium area and a small area.

Line

Lines lead the eye throughout the composition and are a very powerful element of design.

Lines can be defined as formal, meaning they are precise, neat and even, or informal, meaning they are careless, ragged and uneven.

Horizontal lines suggest stability and repose, while vertical lines are uplifting and strong. Diagonal lines are dynamic and when they zigzag are energetic and abrupt. Curving lines are graceful, rhythmic and gentle. Small closely spaced lines and calligraphic lines make pattern and texture. Lines that join and crisscross the surface create shapes.

Abstract line is a visual line the eye follows, created when elements are positioned so the eye hops from one to the other, just as pebbles placed in a row will create a line the eye follows. Patches of contrasting colour, areas of texture or very dark tones across a picture will create a line that moves the eye around the composition.

With onglaze painting lines can be used to emphasise the shape of the piece. Vertical lines up and down a cylinder will make the piece look tall and slender. Horizontal lines around the same piece will act as contour lines and emphasise the width. Curving, spiralling, organic lines emphasise the curves of a rounded piece, whereas straight lines across a curved piece will create a strong contrast and spatial tension which can be very striking.

Shape

Shapes can be defined as geometric, meaning they are created by measurement, such as circles, squares, ovals, oblongs etc., or irregular free form shapes. We have a tendency to draw geometric shapes rather than irregular shapes because of our conditioning in a modern society. Drawing an interesting free form irregular shape can be quite a task. Geometric and irregular shapes are illustrated on the next page. Shapes can have strongly defined boundaries or vague edges.

Groups of objects form shapes such as a shoal of fish, a group of people or a bunch of leaves on a tree.

Shapes can be positive or negative in a design. When an artist creates a design, attention is focused on the positive shapes and lines and background shapes are ignored. However, the spaces in between the shapes and lines create a negative design of their own. Both are important to the composition.

Geometric shape

Irregular shape

Texture

The term texture can include both actual texture, also called tactile texture, meaning 'able to be felt', and implied texture, meaning the effect is entirely visual.

Raised texture on the surface of ceramic creates actual texture. As the light strikes the different levels and angles of the raised texture it creates light and dark tonal effects. Implied texture is flat on the surface and only simulates textural effects by contrast of colour, tone and other design elements.

Texture can be fine, rough, coarse, smooth or linear etc. Tiny repeating dots for instances create a fine texture while spiky shapes create a rough texture. The texture may be regular, meaning the units repeat themselves formally, or irregular, meaning the units vary in size and spacing.

Pattern is formed when units repeat themselves in a sequence and we often find it easier to create pattern than irregular texture.

Onglaze painting methods can produce an incredible number of implied textural effects: pen work, dot work, sponge, plastic wrap pressed into wet paint, streaky brush work and impressionism, to name a few mentioned in previous chapters.

Tone

Tone is the light and dark value of colours. A light toned colour is nearer to white and a dark toned colour is nearer to black.

Gradual shifts from light to dark give the illusion of a curving surface while abrupt changes indicate a change in direction.

The human eye can actually identify more than 25 tonal values between white and black, yet many artists are only aware of three—light, medium and dark.

Tones can be measured by making a one to ten grey scale with black and white paint. White is number one at the top of the scale and the lightest grey is number two. A mid-tone grey is in number five position and the greys become progressively darker until completely black at number ten.

The tones of colours are measured by comparing them with the grey scale. Yellow reflects the most light and at full saturation a lemon yellow will equal number two on the grey scale whereas a deep yellow will compare to number three. By adding black the yellow can be darkened but quickly loses its character; a dark yellow rarely exceeds number five on the tonal scale.

Red and green at full saturation register number five on the tonal scale while violet compares to number seven; even with copious quantities of white added, violet will not lighten beyond a number three value. Proof of this can be seen by photocopying colours and reducing them to grey tones.

Tones can be measured by making a one to ten grey scale

In a picture, dark tones advance and will appear dominant and close. A tree for instance painted in a dark tone on a light background will loom over the scene and impose its presence in the picture. Light tones recede, appearing distant and misty. The theory of atmospheric perspective is based on gradual tonal change from dark at the front to light at the back. To create a feeling of great depth in a picture, the objects furthest from the viewer are painted in light tones, while closer objects are painted in darker values.

The amount of light or dark in a picture or design is referred to as the 'key'. In high key all the tones are nearer to white. These pastel colours create a feeling of tranquillity, innocence and peace, and so are overwhelmingly preferred for interior design. In low key all the tones are nearer to black, giving a feeling of twilight, evening, a rainy day, mystery, dignity and richness.

When all the colour tones, light, medium, dark, black and white, are used in a composition the key is called 'full contrast'. This is typical of a scene in full sunlight with every colour and tone present: patches of bright reflected light, white light and areas of dark shadow. When we paint naturalistic objects and scenes we tend to paint in full contrast key, but many artists forget to use the full range of tones then wonder why the work is lifeless.

The most difficult tonal key to apply is high key as the colours have to be applied very lightly or mixed with white. As onglaze design is built up over a series of firings, there is a tendency to add more and more colour until the delicate high key effect is lost and the tonal qualities become darker. Many onglaze designs begin in tones of full contrast key but due to overpainting and muddy colours end up as low key compositions. Controlling the amount of light and dark in a design requires practice.

Colour

Painting in onglaze colours is not as direct as painting in watercolours, acrylics and gouache. Many colours fade and change during the firing process and it is important to become familiar with your own range of colours by test firing them.

There are very few primary hues in the onglaze range, so basic colour mixing to produce secondary and intermediate hues is complicated. Those artists familiar with colour mixing in other mediums will quickly recognise the clear onglaze colours that can be mixed successfully, but for novices it is advisable to experiment rather than risk mixing a dirty colour.

Onglaze colours are made from minerals and when two different minerals are blended a reaction can occur in the firing process with devastating results. The classic example is trying to mix red and yellow onglaze paint together to create an orange. Some reds are iron based and others are cadmium based. Yellows contain antimony. Mix these minerals together and fire them and the result is a dirty brown. There are special 'mixing yellows' and compatible reds that can be mixed, but the result is not a true orange.

Recognising which colours to mix together comes with experience and by experimentation. I always buy strong clear colours as it is very easy to dull a colour in onglaze.

Light colours can be created by either applying the paint thinly and allowing the white surface to show through or by mixing white into the paint. Thin colour, however, may not glaze very well, whereas a colour mixed with white means a thicker layer of paint can be applied which will fire with a better glaze.

An experienced artist used to working with colour in other art mediums will find onglaze colours limiting. However, the compensation is in the rich glossy finish, the iridescent frosty metallics, the lustres, bronze, coppers and the opulence of shimmering gold and platinum.

Knowing something about colour harmony is the secret of coping successfully with the onglaze colour range. Colours can be grouped loosely into two groups.

'Faces in a Crowd' — Heather Tailor. Painted in eight grey tones plus black and white

Warm colours are those that contain yellow: orange red, terracotta red, red brown, brown, burnt orange, orange, apricot, salmon, ochre, golden brown, gold, deep yellow, lemon yellow, chartreuse, yellow green, olive green, brown green, autumn green and emerald green.

Warm colours advance, the most prominent being red followed closely by orange and yellow.

Cool colours are those that contain blue: blue-green, jade, ming, aqua, turquoise, sky blue, cerulean blue, cobalt blue, royal blue, sapphire blue, delph blue, blue-violet, mauve, purple, red-violet, heliotrope, magenta, maroon, ruby, pink and grey.

Cool colours recede, grey and violet being the two that recede the most.

Red can be either warm or cool. A warm red leans towards orange; for example, orange-red. Most of the compatible onglaze reds are orange-reds. A cool red leans towards blue; for example, magenta, ruby, ruby-purple.

Green can also be either warm or cool. A warm green leans towards yellow; for example, autumn green, chartreuse, yellow-green and emerald. A cool green leans towards blue; for example, blue-green, jade, ming and peacock green.

The warm colours of the onglaze range, excluding the reds, will all mix together quite successfully to create a surprising range of golds and greens.

The cool colours of the onglaze range can all be combined to make a huge range of violets, purples, mauves, pinks and blue-greens. A bright strong ruby colour combined with a royal blue produces either a blue-violet or red-violet depending on the quantities. Blue-green and ruby produce a grey-violet.

When warm yellows, golden browns and chestnuts are mixed with cool violets, purples and ruby colours in the onglaze range, they produce neutral greys. When a colour scheme is either predominantly warm or cool, introduce a neutral colour based on a mix of violet and yellow or gold and purple.

Contrasts

Every artist is familiar with the basic colour wheel. The colours opposite one another are called complementary colours; for example, yellow and violet, red and green, blue and orange. Complementary colours are so called because each colour in a fully saturated state creates an after image of its opposite. When you stare at a strong yellow colour, then look away, you will see violet in front of your eyes. The opposite happens when you stare at a strong violet; the eye creates yellow.

Complementary is derived from the word 'complete' and in art it means that opposite colours complete the cycle. Many artists use only complementary colours as complete colour schemes, mixing the colours together and with black and white to produce hundreds of tints, shades and neutrals.

When complementary colours are positioned next to one another they bathe each other in an after image glow and look much brighter, so bright in fact that the effect can become kinetic and create a visual overload that dazzles.

Unfortunately all colours are not equal in tonal value. Yellow is a much brighter, lighter and intense colour than its complementary colour violet, and will dominate any combination. A more pleasing effect can be produced when the brightest colour of a complementary pair is dulled; for example, dull yellow with a strong violet. Both colours can be dulled or tinted with white and still create a lively exchange.

Many of the colours within the onglaze range are, however, not pure primaries and many of the true complementary effects cannot be employed, for instance, blue and orange. The onglaze blues are quite clean and bright, but the oranges are difficult to produce and are quite incompatible for mixing with blue to produce neutral tones. Red and green are another complementary pair in the onglaze range that will not respond to mixing. However, many of the onglaze paints are unusual colours and if they can be contrasted with their complementary colour will produce very interesting colour combinations.

Contrasting colours create lively colour schemes, and complementary pairs are not the only colours that can be used; there are many interesting colour combinations to be discovered. The warm-cool colour scheme is very easy to use. Any number of harmonious warm colours are used together with one colour from the cool range. Imagine autumn leaf colours of red, ochre, orange, brown, old gold, chestnut, brown-green and green together with ruby and purple. The last two colours are the cool contrasts. The scheme can be reversed, any number of cool colours with one warm colour as a contrast. Look at a peacock for the perfect example of this principle.

Colour is often a matter of strong personal preference, so when you choose a colour scheme there is no guarantee that it will please everyone. Fashion also dictates the latest colour schemes for interior furnishings. As an onglaze artist the dictates of fashion and other people's taste for certain colours can affect the market value of pieces offered for sale at exhibitions. For instance, violet is not a popular colour for interior *objets d'art* and many colours are associated with particular rooms in a home. Because most of the items onglaze painters produce are functional, the use of colour has to be considered, especially if the piece is to be offered for sale. I personally do not let other people's taste and fashion dictate the colours I use on my work and find that eventually a buyer turns up who appreciates the same colours I do, but this is something for you to decide.

In Conclusion

Design is a very broad area and the few pages I have written here are intended as a brief insight.

Art is a life time commitment; creative designers observe and absorb impressions from around themselves. These impressions drop into the subconscious mind and like cells divide and combine to form new entities.

Originality results from individuality and as no two people are alike, so no two designs should be precisely the same, unless you copy.

When faced with the task of having to create their own designs, many of my art students say 'but I can't draw', but what they are really saying is, 'I have no hand and eye co-ordination and I cannot see'. Drawing is the tool of art, it is learning to see the wonderful world of line, shape, texture, tone and colour and being able to translate that information to the hand that holds pencil and brush.

15 Showcase

Fruit in the sgraffito technique (Chapter 10)

'Fremantle Harbour 1900' — 40 cm oval wall plate in pen and wash (Chapter 7)

'Pear Bowl' — 30 cm bowl, metallics on black ceramic (Chapter 10)

Monoprint stencilling with plastic wrap (Chapter 6). This mug was painted with Meissen red and fired, then black paint was sponged onto a tile and a piece of plastic wrap pressed into the paint. The paint-covered plastic film was pressed onto the surface of the mug and removed, and the mug fired a second time

'Pilbara' — 28 cm black ceramic vase with bands of metallic and dribbles. One fire (Chapter 10)

Index